The Kent Ramblers Guide to the
Kent Coast Path
Part 1: Camber to Ramsgate

2

ISBN: 978-1-906494-71-1

Published by Kent Ramblers
www.kentramblers.org.uk

Front cover: Old Parker's Cap from Kingsdown
This page: Sandwich Bay

Contents

4

Introduction

The Kent coast is one of England's national treasures. Instantly recognisable, frequently beautiful, always packed with history and places of interest, it invites and entices visitors to explore. It is no wonder that it is one of the first parts of the new England Coast Path to be opened.

This book describes the route from Camber (just over the Sussex border) to Ramsgate – and also a link route from the nearest station at Rye. As well as providing brand new mapping of the path, it offers a companion to walkers as they tackle all or part of the walk. Clear guidance to the route is given in the commentary, along with insights into the places visited and suggestions for further exploration for those with time to do so.

The Camber to Ramsgate stretch of the coast combines two major physical features; flat lands and the White Cliffs. The resort town of Camber is a gateway to Romney Marsh, a large and low-lying area of land, reclaimed from the sea and made fit for habitation and for agriculture by human effort. It remains an isolated part of the country, but not as remote or bleakly beautiful as is Dungeness. Here is Europe's largest shingle

desert, the driest place in Britain, an area of Special Scientific Interest, and well worth exploring.

Romney Marsh gives way to the pre-Roman coast near Hythe, beyond which the higher land of the North Downs creates the famous White Cliffs. From here there are spectacular views across to France, as well as over the historic towns of Folkestone and Dover.

Along the way, the walk passes places which tempted invaders to land. Romans, Jutes and Vikings all landed along this stretch of coastline. St Augustine landed near Pegwell Bay with the peaceful intent of reintroducing Christianity. Napoleon and Hitler both coveted Britain and their unsuccessful but very public longings produced much visible fortification of the Kent coast.

Apart from protecting Romney Marsh, Government attention has increasingly been directed to fortifying other parts of the coast against the rising sea. The resultant sea walls make for easy and accessible walking.

The modern coast also reveals evidence of fundamental economic and social changes. Silting of the rivers Stour and Wantsum cut off Canterbury's river access to the coast and more significantly Sandwich, which until the 13th

century had been a major port and safe haven for ships. It is now a beautifully preserved medieval town. Similarly, rail and road improvements, coupled with the Channel Tunnel, have favoured Dover, now the world's busiest passenger port. Tourism around the coast has also continued to grow, drawing on ease of access to build on the region's outstanding natural beauty and historic importance.

To walk the Kent Coast Path is to experience a glorious variety of landscapes and to walk through history.

Planning your Walk

Most people are likely to tackle the route as a series of one day walks. Good public transport means that it is easy to get back to your starting point after a day's walking or to manage without your car altogether.

We have not provided details of accommodation for those wishing to do the whole route at one go as such information becomes out of date quickly and is readily available on the Internet.

The maps in this guide, combined with comprehensive new signage for the whole route, should prove adequate for your needs but for a wider perspective you may wish to carry Ordnance Survey 1:25,000 Explorer maps – sheets 125, 138 and 150 cover the whole route.

For route planning purposes it is wise to assume a walking speed of two miles an hour.

Apart from the sections from Folkestone to Dover and on to Kingsdown, the terrain is fairly level and where the route follows the sea wall it has a good surface. Nevertheless, sturdy footwear is recommended even for these sections, especially if you are likely to make a detour onto the sand or shingle.

Refreshments are readily available most of the time over most of the route but it is still wise to carry water and a snack. It is also wise to carry a mobile phone in case of difficulty.

The biggest danger on the walk is when crossing roads.

Don't forget your sunhat, sun cream, sunglasses and camera. If you belong to English Heritage, your membership card may come in useful at Dover, Walmer and Deal castles and Richborough Roman Fort – and at Dymchurch Martello tower in the unlikely event that it happens to be open as you pass. Your National Trust card will get you into the South Foreland lighthouse, the Fan Bay Deep Shelter (but check booking arrangements carefully) and the car park at the White Cliffs Visitor Centre.

About the Kent Coast Path

The path around the Kent coast is just part of a trail being created along the whole of England's coastline. In fact a trail is just one aspect of the Coastal Access Scheme introduced by the Marine and Coastal Access Act 2009 which also provides for access to a wider coastal margin on the seaward side of the trail route (see page 41).

Since the inception of the scheme in 2009 there have been moments when we wondered whether it would survive the economic downturn and changes of government. Thanks to constant and imaginative campaigning by the Ramblers nationally, not only is the project still progressing well but its completion date has been brought forward to 2020 and additional funding has been provided to allow this to happen.

Kent is one of the first counties to benefit from the creation of a section of the England Coast Path. Although responsibility for the path lies with Natural England, much surveying work has been done by Kent Ramblers, in particular by its Coastal Access Officer, Ian Wild. Ian set about walking the full length of the Kent coastline twice, once in each direction. He produced a detailed survey and recommendations which, after endorsement by Kent Ramblers' Area Council, were submitted to Natural England.

We have been delighted with the level of cooperation between Natural England and the Ramblers which we believe has led to the best possible proposals being submitted to the Secretary of State. In truth a lot of the Kent coast was already accessible but the creation of an official path has led to significant improvements in key places and ensured that access everywhere is protected for future generations.

The first section to be considered was from Folkestone to Ramsgate. Although most of the route was quickly agreed, an objection to the

A postcard produced by the Ramblers in 2013 to support the successful campaign to prevent the coastal path becoming a victim of DEFRA spending cuts.

proposed creation of access rights along Richborough Quay delayed final agreement. The inspector responsible for recommending the route to the Secretary of State was initially minded to accept the objection but we in Kent Ramblers felt that the quayside route was a huge benefit to walkers and we campaigned vigorously to retain it. As a result around 60 members of the public responded to the consultation, almost all supporting the quayside route, which impressed the Inspector sufficiently for him to comment on the fact. The final outcome is a compromise whereby the quayside route will in theory be available except when the land-owner specifically requires the land

for storing vehicles. In practice it seems that the quayside will be in use for storage most of the time and walkers forced to use the roadside cycle track.

Meanwhile the section from Camber to Folkestone was finalised and both sections opened on 19 July 2016. This book, covering the whole route from Camber to Ramsgate plus a link route from Rye, is being released to coincide with the opening.

Work is under way on further sections from Ramsgate past Margate to Whitstable and eventu- ally to Gravesend and perhaps beyond. We intend to cover the rest of the route in Kent with a second book once it is open.

Taking the seaside to Westminster: as part of the Ramblers' campaign to save the coastal path, the campaign team took an ice cream van to Parliament where they handed out ice creams and their report on the case for the path to passing MPs.

The Changing Coastline of Kent

The coastline of Kent has undergone major changes over the centuries. In Roman times all of what is now Romney Marsh was sea and the coastline (see map on this page) was just a few hundred metres north west of the route of the Royal Military Canal. The Saxon Shore way is a long-distance walk that follows the ancient coastline along which the Romans built a series of forts to protect against Saxon raids. In those days the Isle of Oxney and the Isle of Thanet were indeed islands. Rye was already a busy port, exporting the products of the Wealden iron industry which may have been one of the reasons for the Roman conquest.

By the thirteenth century a fair bit of Romney Marsh had formed along with a large bank of sand and shingle at Dungeness (see map opposite). New Romney at the mouth of the river Rother was then the major port in the area. However a huge storm in 1287 changed the situation overnight. The mouth of the Rother at New Romney became completely blocked by shingle and New Romney became landlocked.

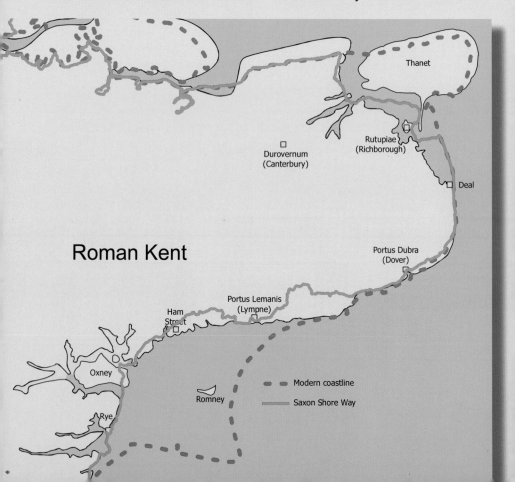

Roman Kent

Thanet

Rutupiae (Richborough)

Durovernum (Canterbury)

Deal

Portus Dubra (Dover)

Portus Lemanis (Lympne)

Ham Street

Oxney

Romney

Rye

- - - Modern coastline
—— Saxon Shore Way

The Rother was diverted past Rye which assumed the role of the principal port in the area, eventually becoming one of the Cinque Ports with a key defensive role against French and Spanish invasion. The storm also destroyed what was left of Old Winchelsea on an island in the harbour – the town was rebuilt on higher ground further west.

Rye Bay around 1200 AD

Tenterden □

Appledore □

□ Dymchurch

Oxney □ Stone

New Romney ▢

Rother

Rother

Rye ▢

The Camber

Old Winchelsea

☐ Land
■ Shingle
☐ Sand
● ● Modern coastline

However, as time went by Rye Harbour gradually silted up and Romney Marsh joined up with Dungeness. Rye is now connected to the sea by a narrow channel and its remaining maritime connection is its fishing fleet.

The Isle of Thanet remained separated from the mainland by the two-mile wide Wantsum channel that linked the English Channel with the Thames Estuary until the end of the mediaeval period. Roman shipping between London and the continent regularly used the Wantsum channel and the Romans built forts at each end, at Reculver (Regulbium) in the north and Richborough (Rutupiae) in the south. The Wantsum gradually silted up and, despite attempts to maintain the channel at Sandwich, the former port (also one of the Cinque Ports) is now some distance from the sea on a loop of the river Stour that forces the coast path along a substantial inland detour.

Small Hythe was once the busy harbour for the port of Tenterden on a wide channel north of the Isle of Oxney

Cycling the Kent Coast

Much of the official route, particularly along sea defences, is shared by walkers and cyclists. In most places there is sufficient room for both types of user without causing conflict but when space is restricted or congested cyclists should always give way to walkers. Cyclists should not attempt to use the footpaths that are for walkers only.

The map opposite shows the national and regional cycle routes as well as a section of sea wall not part of either but in use by cyclists. The route maps for the various sections of the route show these cycle routes as purple dotted lines. In some places where the dotted lines are obscured by other routes, a blue cycle symbol is additionally shown.

From **Rye to Camber** there is a dedicated cycle track further from the Rother and the sea than the route for walkers.

From **Camber to Lydd** the walking route along the sea defences and then along a dedicated cycle track is shared with cyclists.

From **Lydd** there is the option of following National Cycle Route 2 to Hythe but this is well away from the coast so cyclists may prefer to take the Dungeness Road to The Pilot inn and pick up the route from there with the opportunity to visit Dungeness too.

From **The Pilot Inn to Greatstone-on-Sea** cyclists have the advantage of completing a rather dull few miles somewhat quicker than walkers. When the

walking route goes down to the dunes, cyclists continue along the road to Littlestone.

From **Littlestone to Dymchurch** and on to Dymchurch Redoubt, both cyclists and walkers follow the sea wall. From the Redoubt cyclists can take the road into **Hythe** and opposite the Romney, Hythe and Dymchurch Railway station they can follow National Cycle Route 2 all the way to **Folkestone**, sharing most of the route with walkers but cyclists having the option of a route through Lower Leas Coastal Park a short distance further from the sea than the walking route.

From **Folkestone to Dover**, walkers and cyclists part company. Walkers can climb from the harbour to the clifftop above The Warren while cyclists follow National Cycle Route 2 along roads at times but also with a fine off-road section from Capel-le-Ferne to the outskirts of Dover.

From **Dover** cyclists can either take the road past the castle then right into Upper Road to reach the National Trust Visitor Centre or they can follow the walking route to the Centre (pushing their bikes up the path from the harbour). They then follow a lane to St Margaret's at Cliffe from where there is another fine off-road section to Kingsdown and then alongside the walking route into **Deal**. Both routes pass the National Trust White Cliffs Visitor Centre.

National Cycle Route 1 follows the walkers north out of **Deal** as far as Sandown Castle from where it takes a route a couple of hundred metres inland (on the opposite side of the golf course) through the Sandwich Bay Estate then cuts inland to **Sandwich**.

Heading north out of **Sandwich**, cyclists benefit from a dedicated off-road route to the west of the Great Stonar industrial estate while walkers take the footway alongside the road. The routes converge at the A256 from where walkers and cyclists share the dedicated cycle track alongside the main road until the Stonelees Golf Centre. Here walkers take a route closer to the sea while the dedicated cycle track takes a shorter route until the routes converge again at the northern end of Pegwell Bay Country Park.

After the Viking Ship the walkers head for the coast while the cycle track takes a higher route, still with good views of the bay, until the routes converge again at Pegwell and remain together along the clifftop and down into **Ramsgate**.

Link Route: Rye to Camber (4.0 miles)

Although the Kent section of the England Coast Path officially starts at Camber, those travelling by train to Rye may wish to explore the historic town and enjoy the walk from there to Camber. There is alternatively a regular bus service from Rye to Camber, roughly hourly on weekdays and Saturdays but only every two hours on Sundays and Bank Holidays.

Connecting Routes

Quite apart from the England Coast Path, there are five long-distance paths starting at or passing Rye:

- Saxon Shore Way, 153 miles from Gravesend to Hastings
- Royal Military Canal Path, 28 miles from Seabrook to Cliffend
- 1066 Country Walk, 32 miles from Pevensey Castle to Rye
- Sussex Border Path, 150 miles from Thorney Island to Rye
- High Weald Landscape Trail, 90 miles from Horsham to Rye

Start from the town side of the station (cross by the footbridge if arriving from Hastings). Head directly away from the station up Station Approach to Cinque Ports Street (the Cinque Ports pub is on the left) and cross to Market Road. At the top of Market Road turn left along the High Street then first right up Lion Street to St Mary's Church (noting the clock on the tower). At church door turn left and then right to reach the war memorial at far corner of the churchyard. Bear left down to Ypres Tower. To enjoy the view or visit the toilets, go through the arch. But for the walk take the path on the left immediately before the arch and then descend steps

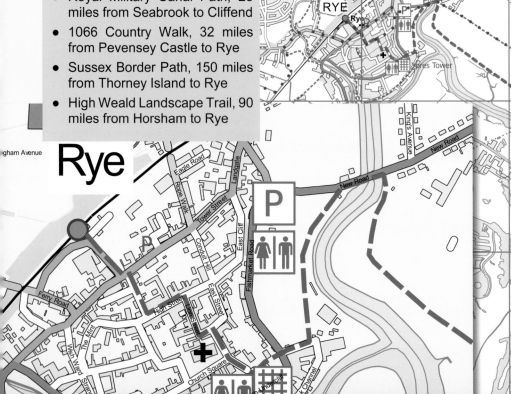

past a pillory and The Ypres Castle Inn.

At the bottom cross the main road very carefully and take track opposite towards the riverside. Turn left along right hand side of park to New Road and turn right over Monk Bretton Bridge across the Rother. Here there used to be the terminus station for the Rye and Camber Tramway and the cycle track that starts here now runs along it. However, the walking route goes through a wooden kissing gate on the right and along the top of a levee with the Rother on the right.

After passing the large Northpoint Beach flooded gravel pit on the left the embankment takes a sharp left turn. The right of way actually goes straight ahead across the marshy and often flooded area ahead but instead take the left turn along a permissive path then a right turn onto a concrete track – keep right along it and note the old rails of the tramway embedded in the concrete. Follow the track to a small parking area – the green building on the left is the former tramway station and on the right is the Harbour Master's lookout. Keep left after the station building along permissive path between fences. After passing the boundary of a garden on your right, bear right back onto the levee alongside the Rother and follow it all the way to the sea and Camber sands. If the tide is out you can turn left along the beach to Camber; otherwise you may have to walk along the dunes – but try not to damage the grasses that hold the dunes together. Immediately after the first buildings, climb up from the beach to the car park where the Kent Coast Path starts (although still in East Sussex).

Public Transport

If you want a bus back to Rye, leave the car park by the main entrance and immediately turn right along a sandy track to the main road. Turn left to the bus stop. Buses (routes 100 and 101) are roughly once an hour on Sundays and Bank Holidays; twice an hour on other days.

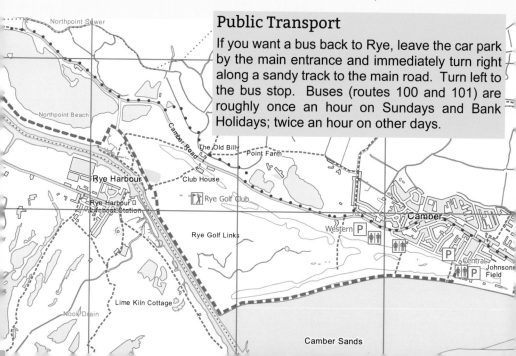

Church of St Mary

Points of Interest from Rye to Camber

Rye

Rye is a charming little town with a rich history reflected in its buildings, walls and layout. From 1287 until late medieval times it was a busy port on a large and well protected natural harbour called The Camber. The harbour gradually silted up and Rye is now connected to the sea only by the narrow channel that carries the Rother and alongside which you can walk from Rye to Camber Sands.

Church of St Mary

The church has graced its lovely setting at the top of the hill since 1150. It was badly damaged in 1377 when the French attacked the town, setting it alight and looting much including the church bells. The townsmen of Rye and Winchelsea launched a reprisal attack the following year, setting fire to two Normandy towns and recovering the bells.

Church of St Mary

The church turret clock (see photograph above) is said to be the oldest in England still running with the original mechanism. It was installed in 1561-62 but opinions vary as to whether it was then new or acquired second hand, perhaps coming from an abandoned Tudor monastery. The clock was substantially overhauled in 2013.

Weather permitting, you can climb the church tower on most days of the year (for a fee) to enjoy panoramic views of the town and surrounding countryside.

Ypres Tower

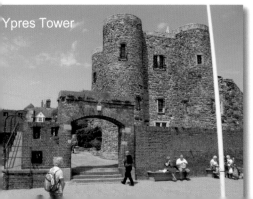
Ypres Tower

The Ypres Tower, one of the oldest buildings in Rye, was built in 1249 to defend against attack from the continent. It now houses a small

Fishing Boats on the Rother

museum that is open daily apart from Christmas Day and Boxing Day

Riverside

Although Rye is no longer a commercial port, it still has a busy fishing fleet and seafood is a speciality in many shops and restaurants.

Lamb House

Georgian Lamb House has been the home of novelist Henry James (from around 1897), the comic writer E F Benson (1917 until 1930) and yet another writer, Rumer Godden who wrote *Black Narcissus* (1968 to 1973). It is now owned by the National Trust and is open to the public on a few days a week.

Rye and Camber Tramway

The Rye and Camber Tramway was built in 1895 to take golfers from Rye to Rye Golf Club. It started not at Rye railway station because the cost of a bridge over the river was unaffordable but at the point where you left the road by Monk Bretton bridge. The 3 ft (90 cm) gauge tramway was extended to Camber Sands in 1908 and the station at Camber relocated in 1938 – but still some way short of Camber village. Used during World War II to convey equipment for the PLUTO pipeline, it never re-opened and was dismantled in 1947. A cycle track now follows the western section of the tramway. The middle section of the route has been destroyed by the now flooded gravel pit on your left. The Golf Links station has been preserved by the golf course owners and there are the remains of some track too.

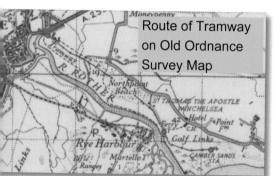
Route of Tramway on Old Ordnance Survey Map

Rye from East Bank of Rother

Camber Sands

Section 1: Camber to Dungeness (9.2 miles)

The Kent Coast Path officially starts in the Central Car Park by the sea front in Camber. Parking in Camber is notoriously expensive so you may wish to organise your trip to avoid it.

This section is easy walking, with no hills, but some parts are actually on the beach, either sand or shingle.

Unusually, there are no opportunities to buy refreshments between Camber and Dungeness, other than by detouring from the route into Lydd. Make sure you have food and drink before leaving Camber.

Make straight for the beach and head east keeping all buildings on your left and the beach on your right. After passing the last building bear a few metres inland and follow the top of sea wall. The sea wall and adjacent beach have undergone major renovation as part of the strengthening of sea defences around Romney Marsh. The works were completed in early 2016 and now provide a broad elevated walkway (and cycle track) giving great views across the seascape to the south and the landscape to the north.

As you approach the end of the sea wall, at the point where the adjacent road bears left, drop down the ramp and cross the road to join the cycle track. (See box for the alternative route along the coast on days when the firing ranges are not in use.)

Dog Walkers

On the very first section of the walk, between Johnsons Field and the beach, dogs are prohibited at certain times of the year. There is an alternative route for those with dogs leaving the landward side of the car park then going around the north and east sides of Johnsons Field to the beach.

Lydd Firing Ranges

It is possible to walk along the coast from Jury's Gap to Dungeness power station but only when the firing ranges are not in use, which is on only about 65 days a year. It is heavy going along the shingle at the top of the beach, so better to walk on the sand if the tide is out.

To find out about range operating times ring 01303 25518 or the information may be available at:

www.hythetc.kentparishes.gov.uk

under Local Information.

The firing range has been used for military training for over 150 years. It includes a mock village used for urban combat training – its fenced perimeter is visible on your right soon after you leave Jury's Gap along the cycle track.

By now, the nuclear power stations at Dungeness, which mark the end of this section, will be clearly visible.

You really can't go wrong from here to Lydd, soon crossing the county boundary into Kent. You no longer have a sea view because the route is heading inland to avoid crossing the military firing ranges. On your left you have fine views of the wind farm which from this distance and vantage point is not without aesthetic appeal. At one point the track kinks away from the road briefly, round the back of a house whose frontage goes right up to the road, and then along the edge of several lakes where water has filled old gravel workings. You are likely to spot many birds and some of the many thousands of sheep on which

On the Cycle Track to Lydd

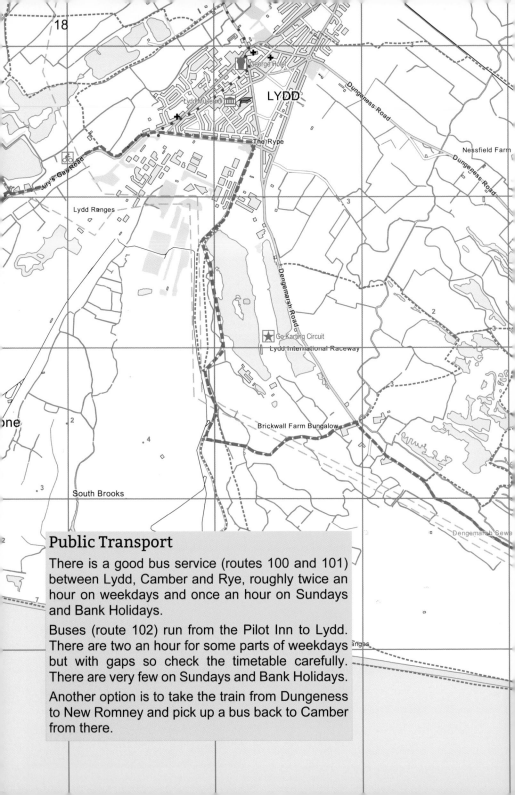

LYDD

George Hotel

Lydd Museum

The Rype

Dungeness Road

Nessfield Farm

Dungeness Road

Jury's Gap Road

Lydd Ranges

Dengemarsh Road

Go-Karting Circuit
Lydd International Raceway

Brickwall Farm Bungalow

South Brooks

Dengemarsh Sewer

Public Transport

There is a good bus service (routes 100 and 101) between Lydd, Camber and Rye, roughly twice an hour on weekdays and once an hour on Sundays and Bank Holidays.

Buses (route 102) run from the Pilot Inn to Lydd. There are two an hour for some parts of weekdays but with gaps so check the timetable carefully. There are very few on Sundays and Bank Holidays.

Another option is to take the train from Dungeness to New Romney and pick up a bus back to Camber from there.

the prosperity of Romney Marsh depended for centuries.

After right and left turns the cycle track crosses the road on the outskirts of Lydd and follows the right right hand verge of the road before crossing it again. There are shops and pubs in Lydd if you need refreshment.

The coast path continues to follow the road round to the right past the army training camp until the road bears slightly to the right; at this point take a concrete track on the right.

Follow this track alongside the meandering perimeter fence of the firing range for about two miles to a junction with an asphalt public road on your left and a farm track straight

ahead. Turn right along more concrete track and follow it, again with firing range fence on your right, all the way to a parking area at the beach.

Turn left along the top of the shingle bank, or the beach if you prefer and the tide is out as the shingle is very heavy going, keeping the nuclear power station on your left. After passing the power station, turn left at the corner then bear right, keeping the old lighthouse on your left.

At this point you could take the Romney, Hythe and Dymchurch railway if running. At the station there is a cafe, newly rebuilt in June 2016, or for alternative refreshment you could head to the Britannia Inn.

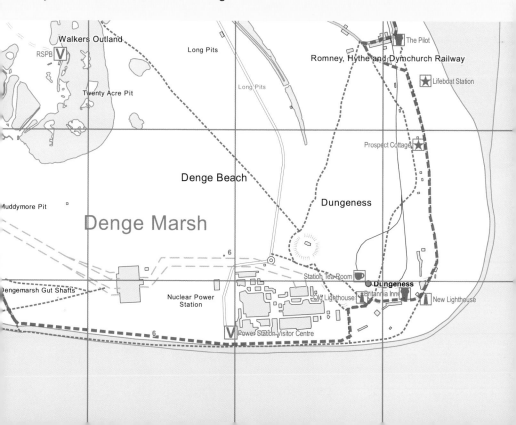

Points of Interest between Camber and Dungeness

Camber Sands

Camber's main claims to fame are the magnificent sandy beach, the only sand dunes in East Sussex (there are plenty over the border in Kent though) and some of the highest car parking charges in the UK outside London. What it cannot boast is Camber Castle which is some distance away to the south west on the other side of the Rother and would perhaps more appropriately be referred to as Winchelsea Castle.

Leaving Cam:

New Sea Defences

The defences from Camber to Jury's Gap were completed in early 2016. They comprise a concrete sea wall and a rock "revetment" on the seaward

Kite Surfing at Broomhill

side of the wall. The rocks have been quarried with dynamite – hence the flat surfaces and the long parallel grooves – and shipped in from as far away as Norway. The defences are part of a larger project covering the coastline from Rye Harbour to Hythe and protecting Romney Marsh, much of which is below sea level, from potentially devastating floods. They are intended to reduce the frequency of such floods from once every 20 years to once every 200 years.

Broomhill

There was once a flourishing port at Broomhill – sufficiently important to be a "limb" of the Cinque Ports. It was washed away by the great storm of 1287 and never rebuilt. It is now a very popular location for kite surfing.

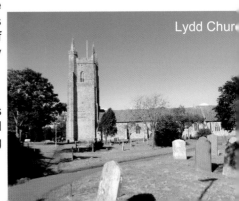
Lydd Chur:

Jury's Gap

This was the site of a massacre of Jews in 1290. All Jews were being expelled from England and a boatload sailing from nearby Broomhill was intercepted by locals from New Winchelsea who robbed the travellers then forced them to disembark onto Jury's Gap, then a sandbank at low tide. When the tide came in they were all drowned.

Little Cheyne Court Wind Farm

The wind farm visible for much of the route from Camber to Lydd consists of 26 wind turbines each 115 metres high (including the length of a blade at its

Wind Farm

highest point). They were erected in 2008 and have a peak capacity of nearly 60 megawatts; the farm is claimed to meet the average annual electricity needs of 33,000 homes.

Lydd

Lydd is an ancient town that for centuries was on the lawless frontier between England and the Continent. Lydd was a port until the storm of 1287 and thereafter its prosperity came from the wool trade.

The church of All Saints, known as the "Cathedral of the Marsh" is the longest in Kent and incorporates the remains of a former Anglo-Saxon church. The 132 ft pinnacled tower, built between 1435 and 1450 although possibly raised to its present height by Cardinal Wolsey when he was merely rector of Lydd from 1503 to 1514, may be the highest of any parish church in Kent with fine vaulting and elegantly carved bosses. Badly damaged in World War II, it has now been fully restored.

Lydd Museum

There is a small museum in the old fire station that is worth a look if passing but check its irregular opening hours first.

The nearby shingle was used for experiments with explosives leading to the development in 1888 of Lyddite, based on picric acid and guncotton.

Authorities differ on the origin of the town's name – some say that it derives from the Old English word "hlid" meaning lid, door or gate while others claim that it derives from the Latin word "littus" meaning shore.

Lydd Airport

Built in 1954 and originally called Ferryfield when it specialised in conveying cars to the continent. That business has moved to the ferries and the

Channel Tunnel so that the main business is now for passengers making the 20 minute flight to Le Touquet. It is sometimes rather misleadingly referred to as London Ashford Airport which is just the name of the company that now runs it.

RSPB Visitor Centre

The roof of the centre is clearly visible on your left from the route between

Power Stations from Shingle Bank

Lydd and Dungeness. It is a bit of a detour but can be visited on foot; or you can drive there later. There are many waterfowl on the drowned gravel pits and hides from which to view them. There are toilets, drinks and a shop selling a wide variety of bird-oriented goods.

Dungeness Nuclear Power Stations

The route follows a shingle bank on the seaward side of the two nuclear power stations. Dungeness A stopped producing power in 2006 and is being gradually dismantled, a process that will not be complete until the reactors are safe enough to remove in 2097. Dungeness B is expected to continue producing power until 2028. For the technically minded, Dungeness A was a Magnox reactor (the design of the first nuclear power stations) and Dungeness B was the first advanced gas-cooled reactor in the UK to begin construction.

There is a visitor centre open free of charge from 9 am to 4 pm Monday to Friday. The centre is not conveniently accessible from the lighthouse area – by car you need to leave the estate, turn left towards Lydd then take the entrance on the left along the white track indicated on the map. Guided tours are also possible but have to be booked three weeks in advance.

Power Stations from RSPB Reserv

Dungeness Old Lighthouse

Old Lighthouses

The black lighthouse is no longer in use but is open to the public at weekends and at other times during the school holidays in the summer months. The round white building is the remains of an even older lighthouse – a wooden structure was once supported by the surviving concrete base now converted into living accommodation.

Dungeness Point

The shingle that makes Dungeness slopes very steeply into the sea, making the bank along the south side of the power stations very popular for sea angling. Cod, sole and bass are commonly caught. From the shingle bank you can see the outflow from the power station "boiling" up not far offshore with, so it is said, 22 million gallons of water every hour being returned to the sea some 12°C warmer than when extracted.

Marsh Frog

Romney Marsh

One of the Marsh's more famous inhabitants is the marsh frog, also known as the laughing frog on account of its irritating call. It was introduced in the 1930s from Hungary to a garden pond near Stone in Oxney from where it escaped and spread throughout the Marsh.

The Sheep of Romney Marsh

After the port of New Romney silted up the marsh lost much of its population and was largely turned over to grazing sheep – as many as 160,000 by 1700. Absentee landowners employed locals who became known as "lookers" to tend the flocks. Although the lookers would normally travel daily from nearby villages, during lambing they might need to stay close to their flocks for several weeks. To accommodate the lookers and their equipment, lookers' huts were built. These were once numerous but now only a few remain.

Lookers' Hut

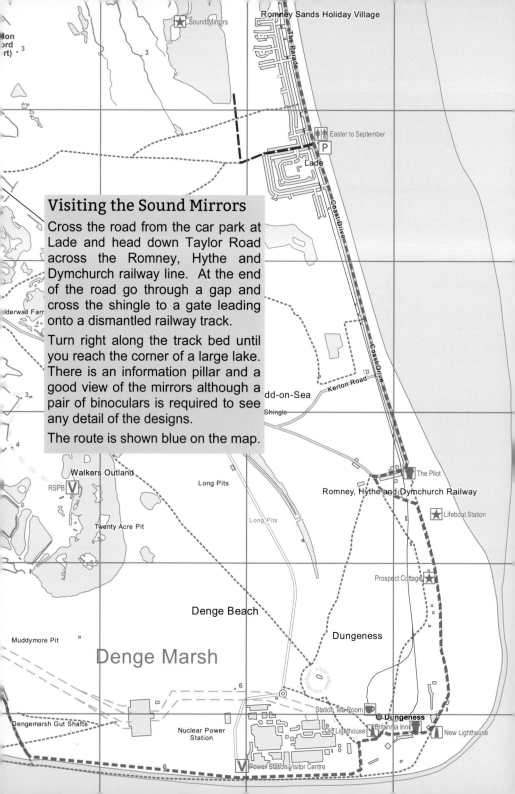

Sound Mirrors

Romney Sands Holiday Village

The Parade

Easter to September

P

Lade

Coast Drive

Iderwall Farm

Visiting the Sound Mirrors

Cross the road from the car park at Lade and head down Taylor Road across the Romney, Hythe and Dymchurch railway line. At the end of the road go through a gap and cross the shingle to a gate leading onto a dismantled railway track.

Turn right along the track bed until you reach the corner of a large lake. There is an information pillar and a good view of the mirrors although a pair of binoculars is required to see any detail of the designs.

The route is shown blue on the map.

dd-on-Sea

Shingle

Kerton Road

Coast Drive

Walkers Outland

Long Pits

RSPB V

Twenty Acre Pit

Long Pits

The Pilot

Romney, Hythe and Dymchurch Railway

Lifeboat Station

Prospect Cottage

Denge Beach

Muddymore Pit

Dungeness

Denge Marsh

Station Tea Room

Dungeness

Dengemarsh Gut Shafts

Nuclear Power Station

Old Lighthouse

Britannia Inn

New Lighthouse

V Power Station Visitor Centre

Section 2: Dungeness to Littlestone-on-Sea (7.0 miles)

Start outside the Britannia Inn at Dungeness.

Head east towards the new lighthouse (the stripy one). Bear left in front of the lighthouse and bear gently left again past a small car park on the left.

Follow the track northwards, noting Prospect Cottage (see note) on your left and the Lifeboat Station (open to the public) on the right. Eventually bear left across the railway, which will remain a companion all the way to Hythe, then right to join the public road near the coastguard cottages on the left. Turn sharp right along Battery Road, crossing the railway again, to The Pilot public house. Buses to Lydd or Camber and to Folkestone stop here.

Bear left along Coast Drive with sea views on the right. The shingle ridge between the road and the beach is part of the Dungeness National Nature Reserve and is a Special Area of Conservation that might be damaged by excessive foot traffic. The ridge should therefore be avoided, and in any case would be very heavy going, but if the tide is out you could walk on the beach below the high water mark. On your left the coastal strip of light residential property masks the view across Romney Marsh.

Continue until you reach a car park and toilets on your right at Lade, where the remains of Lade Fort are visible on the left just after Williamson Road. You could detour down Taylor Road on the left for refreshment – the pub that may be marked on your OS map is now closed but there are a small supermarket and a fish and chip shop. You could also make a detour to view the sound mirrors – see box on opposite page.

Continue northwards to the Romney Sands Holiday Park and the Romney Tavern – Romney Sands Station is just behind the tavern should you wish to catch the RHD train.

Immediately past a white-walled rectangular area on your right, turn right off the road and down to the sandy shoreline (but note the alternative route – see box overleaf) and turn left. A couple of hundred metres past the Greatstone car park (at a point where there may be an artwork made from washed-up rubber gloves) paths through the dunes are available. On a clear day this may be your first opportunity for a view of France.

On reaching the lifeboat station at the southern edge of Littlestone follow the seaward side of the car park then bear left at some large grey metal-roofed huts and follow the track with outdoor gym and children's play area on your left and beach huts in variety of pastel shades on your right. Continue until you reach toilets, the start of a sea wall, a covered look out and a stone drinking fountain at Littlestone. To visit the town of New Romney, including the RHD railway station, head away from the sea along Littlestone Road.

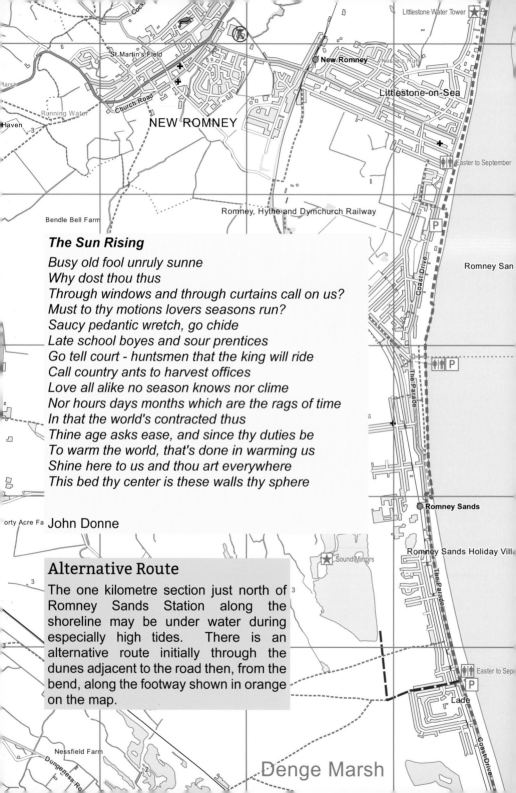

The Sun Rising

Busy old fool unruly sunne
Why dost thou thus
Through windows and through curtains call on us?
Must to thy motions lovers seasons run?
Saucy pedantic wretch, go chide
Late school boyes and sour prentices
Go tell court - huntsmen that the king will ride
Call country ants to harvest offices
Love all alike no season knows nor clime
Nor hours days months which are the rags of time
In that the world's contracted thus
Thine age asks ease, and since thy duties be
To warm the world, that's done in warming us
Shine here to us and thou art everywhere
This bed thy center is these walls thy sphere

John Donne

Alternative Route

The one kilometre section just north of Romney Sands Station along the shoreline may be under water during especially high tides. There is an alternative route initially through the dunes adjacent to the road then, from the bend, along the footway shown in orange on the map.

Points of Interest between Dungeness and Littlestone-on-Sea

Dungeness New Lighthouse

This lighthouse was built in 1961 because the new power station obscured the view of the old 1904 lighthouse.

Marconi Wireless Shed

Just past the Britannia Inn there is a boardwalk leading down to Dungeness point. The new light house is on your left but a few metres to your right you may find, if the dilapidated remains have survived another winter, the shed used by Marconi in the 1890s to conduct experiments into the feasibility of using radio waves as a means of sending and receiving communications. In 1899 he was the first person to send a message across the English Channel, although not from this shed. A year earlier he had sent a signal from the South Foreland Lighthouse (see Section 7) to a ship twelve miles out to sea.

New Lighthouse

Prospect Cottage

Prospect Cottage

Film director, writer and gardener Derek Jarman lived in this cottage until his death in 1994. On the south wall in wooden characters are the first stanza and the last five lines of the last stanza of John Donne's poem *The Sun Rising* which chides the sun for disturbing two lovers in their bed by heralding the routines of a new day. The rear garden features items washed up on the nearby beach and has been the subject of several books.

The Dungeness Estate

Most of the land south of the Pilot Inn belongs to the Dungeness Estate. The road through the estate is privately owned and in 2015 there was talk of making it a toll road. However, in August 2015 the Trustees put the 468-acre estate up for sale at a price of £1.5 million and it was bought by EDF Energy which

Nature Reserve

owns the Dungeness B power station. Designation as a nature reserve and site of special scientific interest severely limits development of the estate.

PLUTO

The "Pipe Line Under The Ocean" was a major war-time project to supply the Allies in Europe with fuel following the D-Day landings. Shipping the fuel across the channel was thought too risky so a submarine pipe line was laid. The pipe line came from Walton-on-Thames and at Romney Marsh it split into two, one part going out to sea at Greatstone and one at Dungeness. The buildings housing the pumps and other equipment to support the pipe line were disguised as bungalows, garages and an ice cream shop. More information can be found in Lydd Museum.

Denge Sound Mirrors

The sound mirrors are concrete structures built in the 1920s to 1930s to focus the sound of incoming aircraft onto microphones placed at appropriate points as an early warning system. The invention of radar made them obsolete before they had been fully deployed. There are other mirrors along

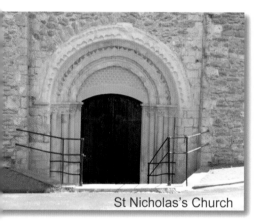

the English coast, including others in Kent, but only here are three different designs found together. The mirrors are on an island in a flooded gravel pit and are accessible only on open days, usually once a year in July. However, a good viewing point can be reached by a 30 minute detour from the coast path at Lade – see box.

St Nicholas's Church

New Romney

"New" Romney is in fact an ancient town. Construction of St Nicholas's Church began in 1080 and took 50 years, the stone being imported from Caen in France. The sea once came right up to the churchyard wall but

Denge Sound Mirrors

since the storm of 1287 the western entrance has been several feet below surrounding land and the adjacent road (see photograph) and the sea is now a mile away.

Having lost its role as a port following the storm, New Romney became an important market town for the sheep that sustained the economy of the marsh for several centuries.

The Cinque Ports

Many towns claim the status of a "Cinque Port" (pronounced "sink", not "sank"), far more than the five that the term implies.

It was Edward the Confessor who first granted Sandwich, Dover and New Romney special privileges – particularly the right to profits from local courts and exemption from tolls and customs duties – in return for providing ships and men when necessary to protect the English Channel and Strait of Dover from any hindrance to the free passage of ships. Hythe and Hastings subsequently joined the confederation, making the original five to which were later added the "ancient towns" of Rye and Winchelsea.

Full members of the confederation were able to share both the privileges and obligations of membership with other towns which were known as "limbs" of their respective "head" towns. The number of limbs varied over the years, totalling perhaps thirty, and included Deal, Ramsgate, Lydd, Tenterden, Faversham, Folkestone, Margate and Brightlingsea (in Essex).

Until Tudor times the ships and men provided by the Cinque Ports were pretty much all that there was of the English navy. The confederation was entitled to send two "barons" to sit in Parliament. Although their obligations had ceased by the start of the 17th century, their privileges were not abolished until 1855.

Tenterden - once a Cinque Port

A Warden, later "Lord Warden", of the Cinque Ports has been appointed since the 12th century to oversee the privileges and obligations of the constituent towns. The now purely honorary title is awarded to individuals who have served the country at the highest level including William Pitt the Younger, the Duke of Wellington, Winston Churchill and the Queen Mother. The official residence of the Lord Warden is now Walmer Castle which is open to the public (English Heritage) where Wellington's room and boots can be viewed (and an excellent afternoon tea consumed).

Swallowtail Bridge

Turnagate Cottage

...gle Hall Farm

Jefferstone Lane

Martello Tower

A259 Dymchurch Road

Apr-Sep

P

St Mary's Bay

St Mary's Bay

P

A259 Dymchurch Road

Romney Warren Halt

Romney Marsh Visitor Centre

Romney Bay House

Marsh Mallow

Romney Warren Golf Course

Littlestone Water Tower

New Romney

Nashe's Run

Littlestone-on-Sea

Phoenix Caisson
(Mulberry Harbour)

Eas

Easter to September

Dymchurch Railway

Section 3: Littlestone-on-Sea to Hythe (10.0 miles)

The first part of this section to Dymchurch and on to the Dymchurch Redoubt follows the sea defence wall. If the tide is out you may prefer to walk on the beach – there are some really fine sands below the high water mark.

Start at the drinking fountain at Littlestone-on-Sea opposite the end of the road from New Romney, erected to commemorate Queen Victoria's Diamond Jubilee in 1897. If you have come by train, turn left out of the station and keep going until you reach the sea front. For those arriving by bus, the stop is just a few metres to the south along the coast road – the 102 service from Folkestone normally runs hourly on Sundays and half-hourly the rest of the week. For drivers there is plenty of parking in nearby roads, especially along the short section of coast road going north before it becomes a private track to the Romney Bay House Hotel.

Leaving Littlestone-on-Sea the most notable landmark is the red brick water tower on the left – see notes. Looking out to sea, note the large rectangular object (or at high tide just the posts at its four corners), the

Mulberry Harbour Caisson – see notes. Continue past the golf course to St Mary's Bay and on to the impressive new sea defences at Dymchurch. On arriving at Dymchurch, pass a Martello tower in the car park on the left then another squeezed between the sea defences and the town buildings.

From here it should be possible to look back and to see Dungeness, whilst ahead the North Downs (on the horizon) and the Greensand ridge (in front and to the left) should be visible stretching eastwards to Folkestone. After a mile or so note a Martello tower on left, apparently converted for residential use, the roof area covered and glazed with 360° views. Continue towards Dymchurch Redoubt, a circular fortification much larger than a Martello tower, that was built at the same time to provide supplies and reinforcements for several towers. Beyond the Redoubt the shoreline passes through the Hythe firing ranges which can be crossed only on the few days a year when there is no firing. The coastal path therefore makes an inland detour to take in a section of the Royal Military Canal.

You could continue to the end of the sea wall at the Redoubt then drop down to cross the road. However, the official route leaves the sea wall

Fine sands at Dymchurch

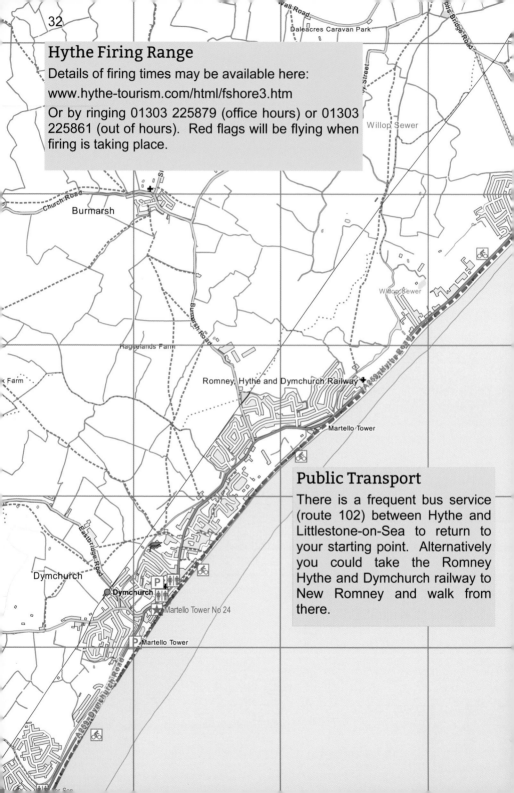

Hythe Firing Range

Details of firing times may be available here: www.hythe-tourism.com/html/fshore3.htm

Or by ringing 01303 225879 (office hours) or 01303 225861 (out of hours). Red flags will be flying when firing is taking place.

Public Transport

There is a frequent bus service (route 102) between Hythe and Littlestone-on-Sea to return to your starting point. Alternatively you could take the Romney Hythe and Dymchurch railway to New Romney and walk from there.

Daleacres Caravan Park

Willop Sewer

Church Road

Burmarsh

Willop Sewer

Burmarsh Road

Haguelands Farm

Romney, Hythe and Dymchurch Railway

Martello Tower

Eastbridge Road

Dymchurch

P Dymchurch

Martello Tower No 24

P Martello Tower

Hythe Ranges

Hythe Ranges

Dymchurch Redoubt

Littlestone Drinking Fountain

rather earlier, soon after passing a holiday park on the left, where there are lay-bys for buses and a pedestrian crossing. Either way, cross the road and turn right along the footway.

After a mile or so, immediately after a petrol station at Palmarsh, take a path down an asphalt track on the left. Pass a water-filled gravel pit on the left and on reaching a heavily fortified gate across the track take a path just to the right at the corner of the fence. Cross the railway and turn sharp right along path close to the railway line. After 100 metres bear left into field then right along field edge, still walking parallel to the railway. There is a recreation area here with seats and a view of a sound mirror on the hill.

At end of the field take the path on the left between gardens into Herons Way (don't let the Kingfisher Gardens street sign confuse you). Bear left to T-junction and turn right along Kingfisher Avenue to T-junc-

tion at end. Turn right but take first opportunity to go through hedge on left to join Royal Military Canal towpath.

Keeping the canal on your left, follow towpath past the Hythe terminus of the Romney Hythe and Dymchurch Railway to road. Cross and continue alongside canal. On reaching next road, bear left to pedestrian crossing, cross and take path down left hand side of Dukes Head public house. Bear left across next road to left hand side of public car park and take diagonal path across The Green. At the far side bear right, keep to left of Hythe Royal British Legion and follow St Leonards Road to sea front, now reaching the northern perimeter of the Hythe ranges.

Turn left along promenade, passing converted Martello tower on left, past swimming pool to a small triangular car park by the Hythe Imperial Hotel.

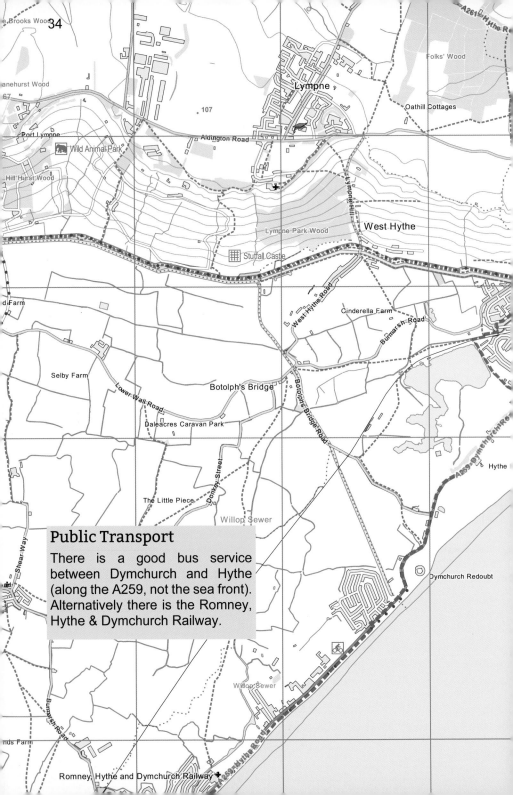

e.Brooks Wood

Folks' Wood

anehurst Wood

67

Lympne

Oathill Cottages

107

Port Lympne

Aldington Road

Wild Animal Park

Hill Hurst Wood

Lympne Hill

West Hythe

Lympne Park Wood

Stutfall Castle

d Farm

West Hythe Road

Cinderella Farm

Burmarsh Road

Selby Farm

Lower Wall Road

Botolph's Bridge

Botolph's Bridge Road

Daleacres Caravan Park

Hythe

Donkey Street

The Little Piece

Willop Sewer

Public Transport

There is a good bus service
between Dymchurch and Hythe
(along the A259, not the sea front).
Alternatively there is the Romney,
Hythe & Dymchurch Railway.

Dymchurch Redoubt

Shear Way

Burmarsh Road

nds Farm

Willop Sewer

Romney, Hythe and Dymchurch Railway

Points of Interest between Littlestone-on-Sea and Hythe

Mulberry Harbour Caisson

In order to support the D-Day landings in June 1944 it was necessary to unload huge numbers of troops and quantities of supplies from large ships. The Allies had access to no harbours large enough for the purpose so they took two prefabricated harbours with them. These "Mulberry" harbours were constructed from a variety of large components, including concrete tanks or "caissons" for use as breakwaters, that were towed across the channel and quickly assembled. Several of the caissons sank or ran aground and remained in place for many decades, the one 1000 metres offshore at Littlestone-on-Sea being there to this day and easily visible from the shore at low tide.

Romney Marsh Visitor Centre

The site is run by Kent Wildlife Trust. The building, accommodating displays and a shop, is designed to be eco-friendly with shingle foundations, straw

bale walls and a living roof. There are several short trails and a reconstructed "Looker's" hut.

Littlestone Water Tower

The Littlestone water tower was built in 1890 as part of a plan for a major expansion of the resort, including a pier that was never built. There were problems with water quality and the tower fell into disuse. It was used as a lookout tower during World War II and is now a residence.

Romney Bay House

Romney Bay House, now a hotel, was designed for American actress and gossip columnist Hedda Hopper by architect Clough Williams-Ellis – more famous for creating the Italianate village of Portmeirion in North Wales which was used as the setting for the 1960s television series *The Prisoner*.

St Mary's Bay

There is nothing ancient about this little town, not even its name. It was not until the 1914-18 War that any significant development took place at what was then the hamlet of Jesson to support a nearby airstrip, with the building of a camp for around 2000 people. After the war some of the buildings were taken over as a holiday camp which developed into a thriving enterprise during the 1930s when the name "St Mary's Bay" was adopted. The holiday camp business declined rapidly in the 1960s and since then most of the camp buildings have been demolished to make way for housing estates.

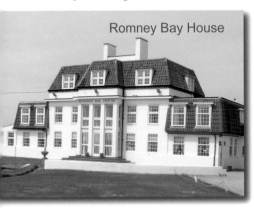
Romney Bay House

Jesson's most famous former inhabitant is probably Edith Nesbit, author of *The Railway Children*. She spent her final years here living with her nautical second husband in two disused army huts that they called "Long Boat" and "Jolly Boat" joined by a passage they called "Suez Canal" – a far cry from the large and magnificent Well Hall in Eltham where she had lived with her first husband. She is buried in the churchyard at St Mary in the Marsh. Her famous book was not, however, inspired by the Romney, Hythe and Dymchurch Railway which was not built until 1927, three years after her death. One of Edith's friends was the young Noel Coward who then lived at St Mary in the Marsh (and subsequently at St Margaret's Bay – see section of path from Dover to Deal). Another was the actress Sybil Thorndike whose brother Russell wrote the Dr Syn books.

Martello Tower No 24

Martello Tower No 24

This is the only fully-restored Martello tower, now in the care of English Heritage. It is normally open only by appointment but occasionally, for example at some bank holiday week-ends, it may be open to casual visitors. The outside can always be viewed at no charge.

Dymchurch Wall

The sea defences necessary to protect a town much of which is around seven feet below sea level were begun by the Romans, reconstructed during

Dymchurch Sea Defences

the Napoleonic Wars and further rebuilt after the great floods of 1953. They have now been even more substantially rebuilt, the latest incarnation being opened in 2011.

Port Lympne

Pronounced "Lim", the estate now houses a zoo, opened in 1973 as an extension to John Aspinall's Howletts Wild Animal Park at Bekesbourne near Canterbury. The house, now a hotel, was begun by local MP Sir Philip Sassoon before World War I and completed in the 1920s.

The Royal Military Canal

Like the Martello towers, the Royal Military Canal was built as a defence against a possible invasion by Napoleon, its 28 miles following quite closely the old Roman coastline. There are frequent kinks in the line of the canal that would have allowed cannon to be fired along the length of a section at any invading army attempting to cross. Even when the canal was being built many doubted its likely effectiveness and criticised the huge cost. Championed by William Pitt the Younger, it became

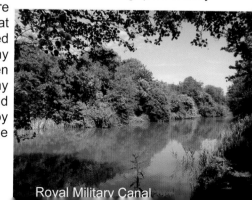
Royal Military Canal

38

known as "Pitt's Ditch". The canal has proved more useful as an obstacle to smugglers and for draining Romney Marsh than as a fortification. Thanks to campaigning and fundraising by the Ramblers, there is a footpath along the full length of what is now a very attractive waterway rich with wildlife.

Palmarsh Bridge and Model Sound Mirror

The coast path passes the southern end of Palmarsh bridge. Across the bridge is a model sound mirror and information board. It is possible for two people to test the operating principle of sound mirrors if one of them stands

Hythe Station

on a platform on the south bank of the canal and speaks quietly while the other stands by the model mirror to hear what is being said.

Romney Hythe and Dymchurch Railway

The 15" gauge railway, the brainchild of Captain J E P Howey, opened on 16 July 1927. It is an exact one-third replica of a normal railway and claimed to be the smallest public railway in the world. Its 5-foot high locomotives are capable of pulling nine coaches full of people at around 25 miles per hour.

Stutfall Castle

The original Roman port, *Portus Lemanis*, was sited here at the then mouth of the Rother, then called the Limen (meaning elm) and hence the names Lemanis and Lympne. Around 270 AD the Romans built a fort here, one of

Hythe Seafront

the Saxon Shore forts built to defend Britain against raids by Saxons and Franks. The other Saxon Shore forts in Kent were at Dover, Richborough and Reculver. The Saxon Shore Way, a long distance walk from Gravesend to Hastings, pioneered by the Ramblers and Kent County Council and which opened in 1980, is named after these forts.

Hythe - Northern Edge of Firing Range

Hythe

The old town is largely built on the steep sides of the cliffs of the pre-Roman coastline. Originally the River Rother passed the site but had been diverted to New Romney even before the Romans arrived. Nevertheless it became a "head" member of the Cinque Ports and provided 11 ships to challenge the Spanish Armada. As shingle has built up the old town has become further and further from the sea with a Victorian seaside resort growing on the newly created land on the seaward side of the Royal Military Canal.

A Venetian Fete is held on the canal every other year (currently in odd numbered years) in August.

St Leonard's Church, Hythe

The church, as well as being large and of considerable architectural interest, is famous for its ossuary – a collection of bones in the crypt (strictly an "ambulatory" for ceremonial procession) under the chancel. There are over 1000 skulls and several thousand thigh bones thought to have been brought here prior to 1500 when dug up from various graveyards in the area that were being commandeered for other uses. The ossuary is open to the public at certain times during the summer months.

Saltwood Castle

On the old clifftop above Hythe, well hidden in the trees, is Saltwood Castle dating from around 1160 although substantially restored in Victorian times after falling into near ruin. Originally famous as the point of rendezvous for the knights who then made their way to Canterbury to murder Thomas Becket, it has since 1953 been the family home first of Kenneth Clark ("Civilisation") and Alan Clark ("Diaries"). The castle was for a time the residence of the Lord Warden of the Cinque Ports, an honour held in recent centuries by Walmer Castle. Now owned by Alan Clark's widow, it is only open for privately arranged tours or on occasional open days to raise money for charity.

Martello Towers

The three Martello towers at Dymchurch are just the first of many that you will pass if you complete the route described in this book. The name comes from Mortello Point in Corsica where the round fortress that inspired the towers is situated.

The towers were built between 1805 and 1812 as a defence against a possible invasion by Napoleon. Originally there were 103 towers on the coast of Sussex, Kent and Essex but many have been demolished so that only 45 now remain, some of these in a poor state. Some towers have been converted for residential use. One of those at Dymchurch has been restored by English Heritage and is open to the public by appointment.

The westernmost two towers at Dymchurch had the additional role of protecting the sluice as the town and much of Romney Marsh are below mean high water mark and could be flooded if the sluice were damaged.

A typical tower was 12m high with walls 2.5m thick (sometimes thicker on the seaward side and thinner on the landward side). The entrance would have been at first floor level with access by a wooden ladder. The flat roof has a parapet and a cannon on a rotating carrier giving it a 360 degree range. Water could be stored in the basement and replenished from rainwater falling on the roof through a system of drains and pipes.

Of course Napoleon never did invade and neither the towers nor the nearby Royal Military Canal, also built to fend off Napoleon's army, were ever put to the test.

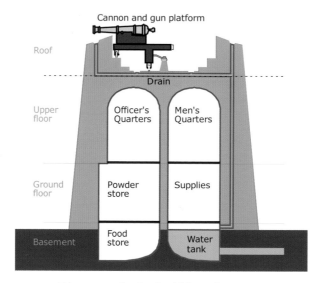

Diagram of a typical Martello tower

Coastal Margin and Spreading Room

The coastal access scheme being implemented by Natural England includes not just the route of the England Coast Path but also additional access rights around the path.

Most people simply walking the path described in this book will not need to know about these additional rights; but for those that are interested they are explained here.

All the land on the seaward side of the path and some on the landward side is designated as Coastal Margin. In the case of the route described in this book, the amounts of Coastal Margin on the landward side of the path are very small and were already accessible by the public. The Coastal Margin on the seaward side is in most cases also very limited as the path is for the most part very close to the water's edge or separated by precipitous cliffs unsuitable for access.

Not all the Coastal Margin is open to the public. Some types of land within the Coastal Margin are excluded from public access. These include buildings, parks, gardens, military land and areas where the wildlife is sensitive to disturbance. Everywhere that the route of the Coast Path lies significantly inland, the land between the path and the sea falls largely into these categories. Thus the amount of Coastal Margin that is not excluded, which is termed Spreading Room, is very small and of little significance to walkers of the path.

Particular exclusions include the military firing ranges and parts of the two National Nature Reserves. Walking north from Dungeness to Greatstone-on-Sea the path is some distance from the water's edge because the unique shingle habitat, part of the Dungeness reserve, is considered too fragile to endure heavy foot traffic and for the same reason is excluded land. This decision will be reviewed after a couple of years. Similarly in the sections from Deal to Sandwich and on to Ramsgate the mud flats and salt marsh in Pegwell Bay are excluded and there are restrictions relating to dogs on the north edge of the bay.

Anyone wanting more details about these additional access rights should look at guidance provided by Natural England:

www.gov.uk/right-of-way-open-access-land/use-your-right-to-roam.

he Cobbler above Dover

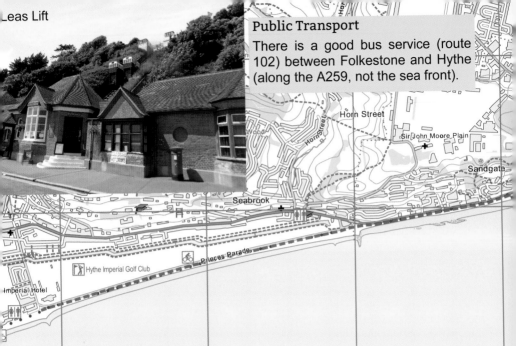

Horn Street

Sir John Moore Plain

Sandgate

Seabrook

Princes Parade

Hythe Imperial Golf Club

Imperial Hotel

Public Transport

There is a good bus service (route 102) between Folkestone and Hythe (along the A259, not the sea front).

Section 4: Hythe to Folkestone (4.5 miles)

Start outside the Hythe Imperial Hotel and head along the sea wall with the Hythe Imperial Golf Club across Princes Parade on your left and the sea on your right. Princes Parade may be a convenient place to park if required.

Pass the car park at the eastern end of the Royal Military Canal on your left, noting its tame end at the sluice gates, and Battery Point on your right. The route is now alongside the main road, initially separated by a fence but soon along a footway on the landward side of the sea wall. On reaching buildings on the seaward side of the road at Sandgate, bear right along the seaward side of the buildings along the sea wall (shared with cyclists). Note Sandgate castle as you pass, built

by Henry VIII to protect a vulnerable part of the coast. Almost immediately, up the hillside, you will notice a modern building standing in a park; this is the headquarters of Saga, one of Folkestone's largest employers.

After passing some rows of beach huts on left, pass the concrete breakwater with children's play area on right. Continue along the sea wall, bearing gently left with Lower Leas Coastal Park on your left. At the end of the Coastal Park, with the cliff lift on your left, continue along the asphalt track near the shoreline to a work of art in the form of a bell hanging on a rope. Immediately after this masterpiece turn left away from the sea to the road and turn right. At the port entrance follow the road left and then right around the marina. Keep to the edge of the marina, go under the railway arch

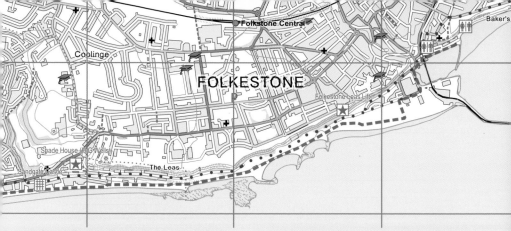

and continue along the quayside to complete this section of the walk at the East Pier. From here you can look back and see the old Folkestone Harbour railway station. In its heyday it was the gateway to the continent for trains from London to Paris, but was closed for normal services in 2001.

Points of Interest between Hythe and Folkestone

Hythe, Sandgate and Folkestone

The three towns give their names to rocks of the Lower Greensand formation that form a ridge running parallel to but south of the North Downs and reaching the coast at the towns indicated. Along the ridge from Haslemere to Hamstreet runs the Greensand Way, a fine long-distance walk devised by the Ramblers in the 1980s. Although it is often said that the Greensand rocks are neither green nor sand, being partly a brownish limestone laid down in a shallow marine bay, they do also contain sand and may be greenish when first exposed to the air.

Spade House

Now a nursing home called Wells House, this was the home of H G Wells from 1899 to 1909. He had the house built to his specification by architect C F A Voysey who was an admirer of Augustus Pugin (see section of walk from Sandwich to Ramsgate). Here he wrote many of his best known books into which he incorporated nearby locations and hosted a literary circle who lived in the area including Edith Nesbit (Dymchurch), Henry James (Rye) and Joseph Conrad (Hythe). Some commentators hold that this "Romney Marsh Group" was as influential as the better-known Bloomsbury Group.

Sandgate Castle

The remains of the castle are on the sea front. Originally built by Henry VIII in 1539 to a ground plan very similar to Walmer and Deal, it was altered in 1806 in preparation for a feared invasion by Napoleon, the central building now having the look of a Martello tower. In 1888 it was sold to the South

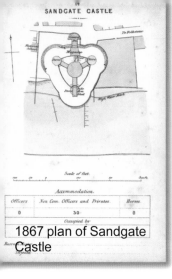

Scale of feet.		
Accommodation.		
Officers	Non Com. Officers and Privates	Horses
0	30	0
Occupied by		

1867 plan of Sandgate Castle

Eastern Railway which planned to use it as a railway station. There was then a line from Sandling through Hythe to Sandgate and the company planned to extend this along the coast to Folkestone. The plan was never realised and the castle has been restored for use as a private house.

Lower Leas Coastal Park

The park is on the landward side of your route as you approach Folkestone. The site was created by a landslip 1874 and from 1828 to 1973 there was a toll road along the bottom of the cliff. From 2000 to 2006 the park was redeveloped using many millions of pounds from lottery funding and European Union and other development grants. The park has won many design awards and is maintained by Shepway District Council.

William Harvey

Above the Lower Leas Coastal Park stands a statue of William Harvey looking out across the English Channel. Harvey was born in Folkestone in 1578, became personal physician to Charles I and is famous for discovering the circulation of the blood. The significance of the work lies not just in the facts that Harvey established but also in the use of something approaching the modern scientific method to do so, one of the earliest examples of hypothesis, experiment and deduction in the history of science.

Folkestone Artworks

The Folkestone Triennial has been held every three years from 2008 as a showcase for newly commissioned public art from nationally and internationally renowned artists. Some of the artworks from each event remain in Folkestone with several alongside your route.

Leas Lift

The lift up the cliff from the eastern end of the Coastal Park has narrowly escaped permanent closure several times in recent years and has undergone several periods of temporary closure for renovation work. First opened in 1885, it claims to be one of the oldest water lifts in the UK. The two cars are linked by a cable passing over a pulley at the top and the weight of one car going down provides the force needed to raise the other. To make the downward car slightly heavier it carries a quantity of water that is released at the bottom and pumped back to the top for re-use.

Lower Leas Coastal Park

Some Folkestone Artworks

Smuggling in Kent

The Kent coast has a long history as the backdrop to smuggling. The activity, involving the illegal import or export of goods (or, less often, people), flourished during periods when high duty was levied. Smuggling was easiest where goods were of high value and small size, but over the years included items such as wool, silk, alcohol, tobacco, gold and spices.

Kent's proximity to continental Europe made it the obvious place for smugglers to engage in their dangerous international trade. Romney Marsh and Deal acquired notoriety in the eighteenth century for their role in the activity, which only fell back with reduced duties coupled with increased policing by Coast Guards from the 1830s.

Few physical signs remain of the smugglers' work. By nature covert and fleeting, it left few signs. However, many pubs and some large houses and some churches still have passages and storage areas believed to have been created and used by smugglers. Literature has celebrated and romanticised smugglers; in Kent the best-known smuggler remains Russell Thorndike's creation, Dr Syn.

As recently as May 2016 Dymchurch was in the news because a boat carrying smuggled immigrants had to be rescued offshore.

The Geology of the Kent Coast

Perhaps the most noticeable thing about the Kent coastline is its variety from the flatness of Romney Marsh to the towering cliffs between Folkestone and Deal. Landscape usually reflects geology and the coastline of Kent is no exception.

The underlying rocks are almost all from the Cretaceous period, roughly from 145 to 65 million years ago. Slightly younger are the Thanet sands which separate Thanet from the rest of Kent and which were largely under the sea until Saxon times. The exception, of course, is Romney Marsh which did not exist in Roman times and is made of recently deposited gravels.

Thanks to continental drift, or plate tectonics, Britain has moved around the globe and for most of its established geological history it has been well south of its current location. During Cretaceous times it was around 10° further south.

The rocks in the diagram below were laid down only during periods when what is now Kent was under water. The oldest rocks are to the left (south west) and the newest to the right (north east). The Wealden sandstone and clay were laid down in a large freshwater lake. The sea then broke through so that the Greensand and Gault were laid down in marine conditions – the former in shallow water and the latter in deeper water. Sea level then rose significantly so that the chalk was formed in deep, warm waters from the calcite bodies of tiny marine invertebrates. Some of the marine inverte-brates had shells of silica and this material became concentrated by a process that is not fully understood into flint nodules that are often found in chalk or in the mixture of clay and flints often found on the top of chalk ridges.

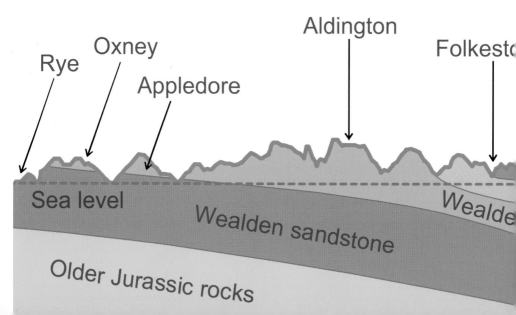

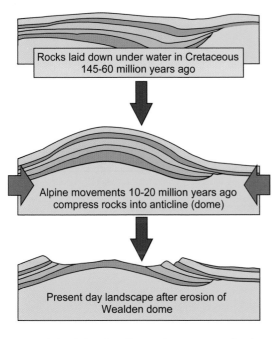

Rocks laid down under water in Cretaceous 145-60 million years ago

Alpine movements 10-20 million years ago compress rocks into anticline (dome)

Present day landscape after erosion of Wealden dome

Younger rocks were laid down on top of the older ones and then the whole formation squeezed into a dome by the earth movements that created the Alps. Erosion then expose the older layers in the centre of the dome. The profile of the coast from Rye to Ramsgate at the bottom of the page represents just one half of the roughly symmetrical dome, the middle being to the left of the diagram.

There are of course plenty of older rocks beneath the strata that actually outcrop at the surface, including the carboniferous limestone bearing the coal seams that used to be exploited by the Betteshanger coal mine – now the Betteshanger Country Park (shown as the Fowlmead Country Park on older maps).

The diagram shows the geological make-up of the pre-Roman Kent coast (i.e. omitting Romney Marsh) from Rye on the left to Margate on the right. The diagram is not to scale and in particular the vertical scale is greatly magnified.

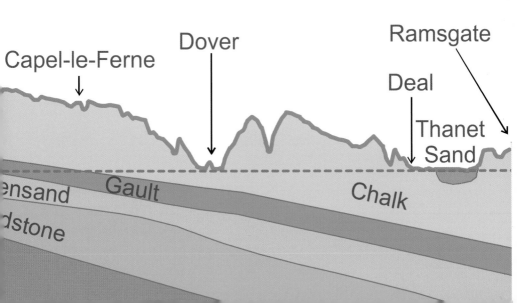

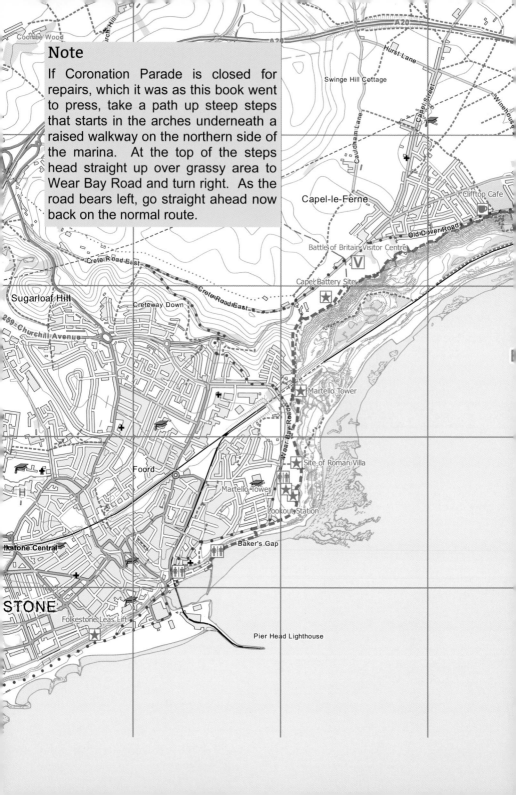

Note

If Coronation Parade is closed for repairs, which it was as this book went to press, take a path up steep steps that starts in the arches underneath a raised walkway on the northern side of the marina. At the top of the steps head straight up over grassy area to Wear Bay Road and turn right. As the road bears left, go straight ahead now back on the normal route.

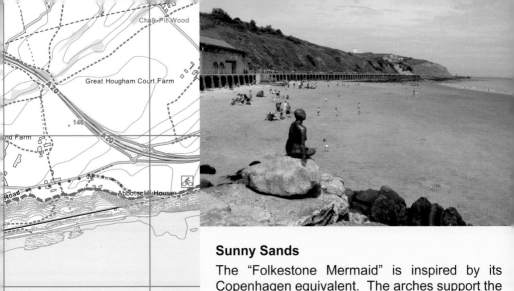

Sunny Sands

The "Folkestone Mermaid" is inspired by its Copenhagen equivalent. The arches support the Coronation Parade and on the horizon are a Martello Tower and the Coastwatch lookout station.

Section 5: Folkestone to Dover (8.0 miles)

Starting at the marina, go through the market area, under the railway and along the quayside to the East Pier. Bear left past Sunny Sands then right past toilets (Easter to September only) and along Coronation Parade above a series of arches as far as you can go. Climb some steps on the left to a grassy area and turn right past many benches and the harbour church. Just before the asphalt track ends at a stone shelter, climb a grassy bank on the left keeping to the right of the National Coastwatch station (which you may be able to visit) and a white Martello tower.

Continue past toilets on your left and an information board on the site of a Roman villa. Bear left to join a track and pass to the left of a second Martello tower. Follow this track over a concrete bridge and climb steeply towards the clifftop. When the path levels out at a T-junction, turn right to reach the cliff edge. Turn left along the coastal path (waymarked Saxon Shore Way). The fenced area on your left is the Capel Battery Site (see box) followed by the Battle of Britain Memorial Garden and the new visitor centre.

Continue along the coastal path, which has a few ups and downs, until you reach a car park by a café. Here steps lead steeply downwards into the East Cliff and Warren Country Park – but do not go that way. Continue along the clifftop road to the left of the café and back onto the coastal path (still the Saxon Shore Way). On approaching a large white building (Abbotscliff House) there is a choice of route –

the Saxon Shore Way goes inland for a while to the left of the white building (Abbots Cliff House). But the coast path follows the seaward side of the building – there are dizzying drops below but there are also railings to keep you safe.

At an old concrete gun emplacement bear left onto an asphalt track (also a cycle route) and turn right past another sound mirror. When the cycle route goes through a gate, turn right for a few metres then left through a gate with a fence on your right. Pass a ventilation shaft for the railway tunnel below, pass the remains of a few wartime buildings and soon there are fine views of Samphire Hoe Country Park below and of ships sailing in and out of Dover harbour ahead. After a

descent there is another ventilation shaft for the railway tunnel, and to your left you can see the main road and a junction where the road to Samphire Hoe goes into a tunnel. If you wish to make a detour to the Hoe you will have to go over a stile here and across a field to the tunnel. Otherwise, or on returning from the Hoe, carry on up the cliff path – with fine views of France on a clear day.

On approaching Dover the path becomes metalled. Take the first turning on the left under the road, still following the Saxon Shore Way (and the North Downs Way). On the other side turn right then left up King Lear's Way and right along Kings Rope Walk. At the end bear left and take a path that initially climbs steeply to a children's play area then

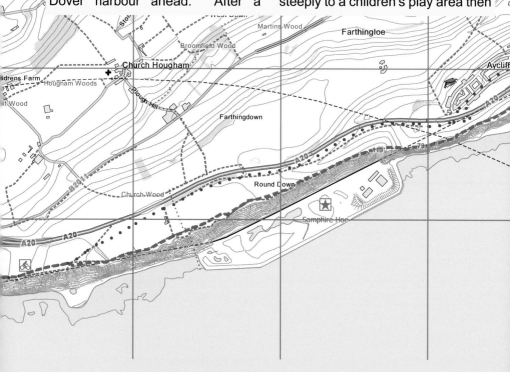

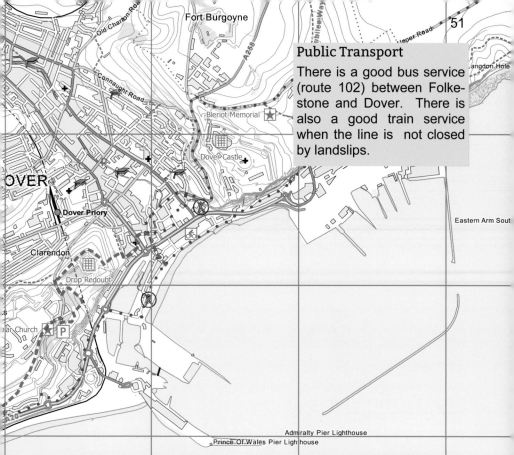

Public Transport

There is a good bus service (route 102) between Folkestone and Dover. There is also a good train service when the line is not closed by landslips.

bears right and climbs more gently to an asphalt track. Bear right past the remains of a Knights Templar Church and down to a T-junction.

Turn right then left across road into car park. Take path at left hand corner between remains of fortifications on your left and fence on right. Turn right down steps and along path to kissing gate. Bear left down slope to another gate. Turn left up broad grassy track with shallow steps and at post and information board just before steeper steps turn left. Ascend concrete steps to lane, turn left to T-junction with road, cross and turn right downhill. At bend take path across road through gate up steps climbing steep grassy bank. Follow this path round the fortifications known as the Drop Redoubt, built from 1805 to 1810 in case of invasion by Napoleon. On reaching a gate offering entrance to the fort, turn left down steps leading into town and to the A20. Cross at some lights a few tens of metres up from the roundabout and continue into the pedestrianised area. Turn right through tunnel under road to sea front at the Channel Swimmers Monument.

Points of Interest Between Folkestone and Dover

Folkestone Artworks

There are more artworks at the Dover end of Folkestone. On the wall by the road to the west of the railway arches is a large map of Europe (pictured) showing the 31 water related walks made by artist Hamish Fulton during his 40 year career.

Coastguard Lookout

The observation station you pass as you climb out of Folkestone up the East Cliff is one of around 46 that have been set up since many of the smaller Coastguard stations were closed down in the 1980s. They are run by a charity, the National Coastwatch Institution, and manned by volunteers.

The station is manned only during daylight hours and visitors are normally welcome to ring the intercom for a look inside and a chat with those on duty.

Roman Villa

Just beyond the observation station, past the Martello tower on the left, a grassy area marks the site of a Roman villa. The villa was discovered in 1923 when exposed by coastal erosion. It was partially excavated in 1924 and until around 1957 the site, with mosaic floor, was open to the public but it was then buried again for protection. There were further excavations in 1989 and in 2010 and 2011 when the project was designated 'Rescue Dig of the Year' by *Current Archaeology* magazine because of the threat of loss through coastal erosion. Beneath the villa is evidence of an iron age settlement including coins and fragments of wine jars.

The Warren

See page 56.

Capel Battery Site

On reaching the clifftop after the steep climb from the Martello tower you will pass a fenced area on your left. This was the site of an extensive network of tunnels and buildings including an underground hospital during World War II. The area is in fact access land which means that, despite the fence, the public can explore it at will. The landowner has from time to time attempted to exclude the public from the site but vigilance by the Ramblers and legal action by Kent County Council have ensured that most of it remains open. However, the site's wartime legacy means that there may be hazards in the rougher areas and walkers are advised to keep to the paths.

Battle of Britain Memorial and Visitor Centre

The large statue of an airman sitting on a huge propeller-shaped structure has been here for many years. The "Wing" visitor centre is new, opened in 2015, offering refreshments and information. There are replicas of a Spitfire and a Hurricane (pictured).

Hurricane at Battle of Britain Memorial

Saved Path

Path Beneath Abbots Cliff House

This path, perched on a slope above the cliff edge, was originally created for use by the authorities based at Abbots Cliff House to watch for smugglers. It offers spectacular views of Folkestone Warren and although the seaward drop is steep, robust railings ensure safety and confidence. In 2002 there was an attempt to close this path but the Ramblers fought a court case to keep it open. The judge who found in favour of retaining the path described it as "a gem".

Sound Mirror

Soon after the Abbotscliff path there is another sound mirror. See page 28 for more information about sound mirrors.

Flora Calcarea

Soon after the sound mirror you may spot in the grass on your right a bronze cast resembling the pages of an open book showing on each page a sketch of a local flower and its pollen grain. There are supposedly eight of these artworks by Rob Kesseler along the cycle route from Folkestone to Dover but, as the cycle route only briefly coincides with the coast path, walkers will not find them all.

Flora Calcarea

Shakespeare Cliff

The cliff is 300 feet high and named for a reference to the site in Shakespeare's *King Lear,* described by Edgar to his blind father thus:

> *Come on, sir. Here's the place. Stand still. How fearful*
> *And dizzy 'tis to cast one's eyes so low!*
> *The crows and choughs that wing the midway air*
> *Show scarce so gross as beetles. Halfway down*
> *Hangs one that gathers samphire—dreadful trade!*

Samphire Hoe

Six-spot Burnet Moths
Shakespeare Cliff

This flat area beneath Shakespeare Cliff was created with five million cubic metres of chalk marl produced as spoil when boring the Channel Tunnel. It houses the ventilation unit for the Tunnel as well as a visitor centre and 2 km of nature walks, especially suitable for wheelchair users. The name derives from the rock samphire found in the area and mentioned in the preceding quotation from King Lear. Not to be confused with the more readily available but unrelated marsh samphire, rock samphire is related to fennel and often pickled – it is said to be a fine accompaniment to both fish and lamb. Access is via a tunnel through the cliff from the A20 westbound carriageway.

The Hoe also helps to protect the Folkestone to Dover railway from slippage. This section between Abbot's Cliff Tunnel to the west and Shakespeare Tunnel to the east was created in 1843. A major engineering achievement, an unstable cliff face had to be removed using 8 tons of gunpowder packed into chambers in the cliff. Crowds gathered to watch the explosion, many from steamships chartered for the purpose. Around a million tons of chalk had then to be removed.

Samphire Hoe

Channel Tunnel Attempts and the Discovery of Coal

Today's Channel tunnel is the result of the latest of several attempts to create an underwater crossing. The first was in the 1880s when shafts were sunk at both Abbot's Cliff and Shakespeare Cliff from which boring machines running on compressed air started cutting their way towards France. Another tunnel was begun from Sangatte in France with the aim of the two meeting in the middle. However, the government started worrying that the tunnel might facilitate an invasion and called a halt to the project.

Pyramidal Orchid

The Channel Tunnel Company then took the opportunity to drill some boreholes to test the theory that a coal field lay beneath Kent's more recent rocks strata with the result that in 1890 they discovered both coal and iron ore. Shakespeare Colliery was established on the site but there were problems with flooding and gas explosions, leading to closure in 1921. However, the discovery led to further exploration elsewhere in Kent with the result that more successful collieries were established, the last to close being Betteshanger near Deal – the site is now the Betteshanger Country Park (previously known as Fowlmead Country Park).

Chalk Lines

Descending from Shakespeare Cliff you will pass a post promoting a series of ten poems by Ros Barber. The posts are mainly on the Dover-Folkestone cycle route (the Chalk and Channel Way) but a few are on the coast path. The displayed telephone number for hearing the poems no longer works but you can listen to them on the Sustrans web site.

Knights Templar Church

Not everyone is convinced that this small church was built by the Templars. The 12th century ruins were discovered during the construction of the Western Heights military defences in 1854. Some claim that it is the site of a meeting between King John and a papal legate in 1213 at which the King's long-running dispute with Pope Innocent III was resolved.

The Western Heights (Drop Redoubt)

These extensive fortifications built deep into the chalk downs above Dover were started in 1779 when England was at war with France and Holland and feared invasion. They were further developed during the Napoleonic wars from 1804 to 1815 and strengthened again in the 1850s and 1860s when tension between England and France was high once more. The cost of the deep ditches and extensive brickwork was astronomical and much criticised. The defences never saw action and are now a home to wildlife typical of chalk downland.

Western Heights

Folkestone Warren

Folkestone Warren is an area of landslip lying at the foot of the chalk cliffs between Folkestone and Abbotscliff. 2.7 km long by up to 350 metres wide, it is an area of interest to geologists, naturalists and naturists.

The cause of the frequent landslips is the thin layer of gault clay near the base of the cliffs. Water percolates down through the permeable chalk until

The 1915 Landslip

it reaches the upper side of the impermeable clay. Similarly water is forced up through the permeable greensand until it reaches the lower side of the clay. The clay is thus well-lubricated and, with the weight of chalk pressing down upon it, has a tendency to be squeezed out onto the beach, causing collapse of the chalk above.

The frequent movements of rock and clay in the Warren are a particular problem because the main railway line from Folkestone to Dover runs through the Warren and has several times been disrupted by landslips. The route was known to be unstable when the railway was built in 1844 but nevertheless adopted because the company was in a race against a competing company to reach Dover and secure continental traffic coming through the port. The worst slip was in 1915 after which the line was closed for four years.

There have been proposals to divert the line but they have always been deemed too expensive and instead the problem has been managed by a series of engineering works. These include drainage, barriers to prevent infiltration by seawater, a concrete apron, a sea wall and the placement of large boulders to reduce erosion and undercutting by the sea. The railway is also protected by a "chalk fall fence" to which a tension-sensitive wire is attached that will turn signals to danger if struck by falling rock.

At the time of writing in autumn 2016 the line has just reopened after a nine month

The Path to the Café

closure, this time due to a collapsed sea wall at Shakespeare Beach closer to Dover. A new 235 metre long viaduct has been constructed at a cost of nearly £40m to replace one originally built in the 19th century.

The Warren was originally grazed as downland but in 1924 the then owner Lord Radnor gave the site to Folkestone Corporation on the condition that grazing cease. In consequence scrub has taken over and a way is being sought to re-introduce grazing by cattle. Meanwhile the dense vegetation makes The Warren an interesting place to explore with its lush woodland and steep paths to the clifftop. It is both a local nature reserve and a site of special scientific interest.

There are paths through the Warren. Access is easiest from the track past the Martello tower at the western end. From the cliff-top café at Capel-le-Ferne a path zigzags down the cliff face to the lush vegetation below. At the eastern end of the Warren another path leads steeply from the top to the bottom of the cliff.

The beach at the eastern end of the Warren was once popular with nudists but no recent sightings have been reported.

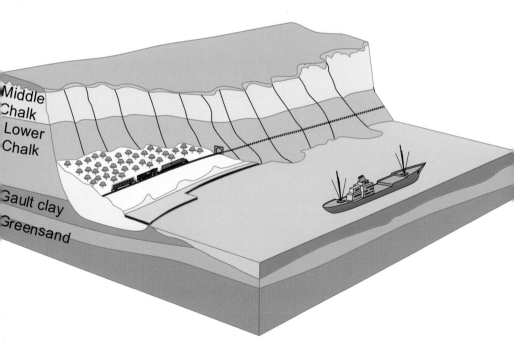

Middle Chalk
Lower Chalk
Gault clay
Greensand

Section 6: Dover to Deal (9.5 miles)

Start at the water's edge looking out across Dover harbour by the Channel Swimmers Monument. Turn left along the waterfront until you reach a pedestrian and cyclists' crossing of the busy A20. Cross both carriageways and turn into East Cliff, climbing gently. At the top just carry straight on as the pavement leads to a path, still climbing steadily and passing under the A2. Pass a kissing gate and keep climbing up steps until you reach the road near the entrance to the National Trust Visitor Centre. Take path through gate on right and take highest path below the fence. After passing through a small patch of woodland the Visitor Centre will be visible up an open slope on your left, offering a detour for toilets and refreshment

Emerging through gate onto open downland, bear uphill and along broad track. As the vista of Langdon Hole comes into view, bear left taking the very clear track that follows a large semicircle to the cliff edge at the far side. Continue to follow clear track until Fan Hole comes into view. Follow path past the entrance to the National Trust's World War II tunnels complex. Follow path around Fan Hole and then parallel to cliff edge. South Foreland lighthouse will come into

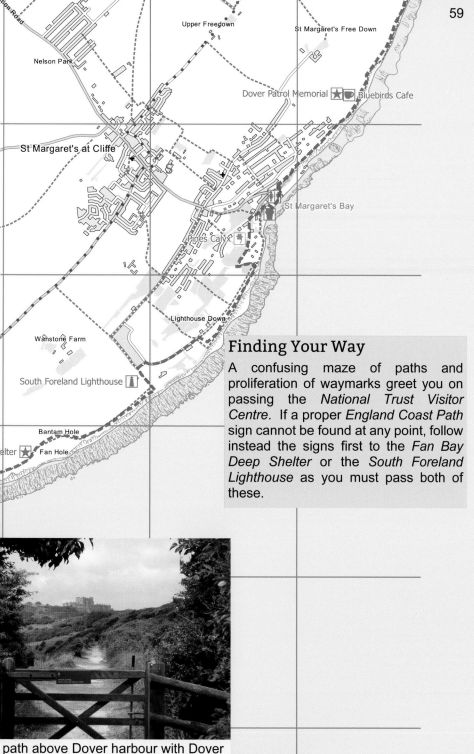

Upper Freedown

St Margaret's Free Down

Nelson Park

Dover Patrol Memorial ★ 🛡 Bluebirds Cafe

St Margaret's at Cliffe

St Margaret's Bay

Pines Calyx

Lighthouse Down

Wanstone Farm

South Foreland Lighthouse 🏠

Bantam Hole

elter ★ Fan Hole

Finding Your Way

A confusing maze of paths and proliferation of waymarks greet you on passing the *National Trust Visitor Centre*. If a proper *England Coast Path* sign cannot be found at any point, follow instead the signs first to the *Fan Bay Deep Shelter* or the *South Foreland Lighthouse* as you must pass both of these.

path above Dover harbour with Dover Castle in the background

The Butts

Kingsdown

White Farm Cottage

Kingsdown Wood

Hill Farm

e Lynch

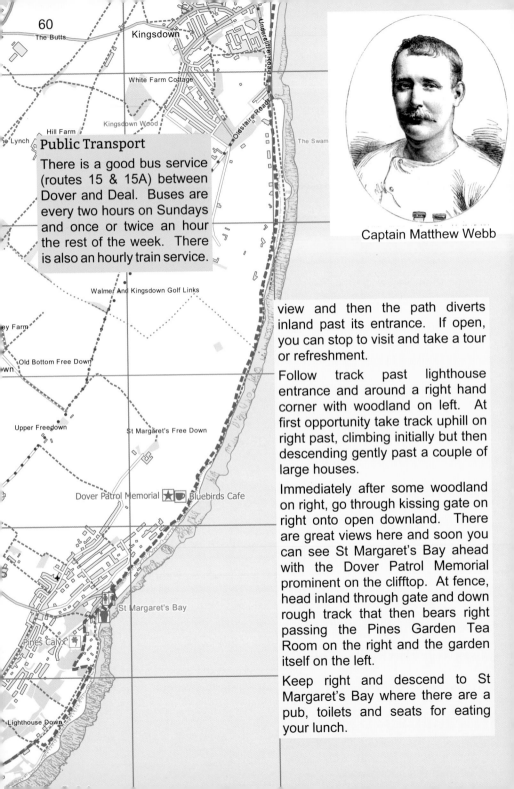

Captain Matthew Webb

The Swam

Public Transport

There is a good bus service (routes 15 & 15A) between Dover and Deal. Buses are every two hours on Sundays and once or twice an hour the rest of the week. There is also an hourly train service.

Walmer And Kingsdown Golf Links

ey Farm

Old Bottom Free Down

wn

Upper Freedown

St Margaret's Free Down

Dover Patrol Memorial ★ ▣ Bluebirds Cafe

St Margaret's Bay

Pines Calyx

Lighthouse Down

view and then the path diverts inland past its entrance. If open, you can stop to visit and take a tour or refreshment.

Follow track past lighthouse entrance and around a right hand corner with woodland on left. At first opportunity take track uphill on right past, climbing initially but then descending gently past a couple of large houses.

Immediately after some woodland on right, go through kissing gate on right onto open downland. There are great views here and soon you can see St Margaret's Bay ahead with the Dover Patrol Memorial prominent on the clifftop. At fence, head inland through gate and down rough track that then bears right passing the Pines Garden Tea Room on the right and the garden itself on the left.

Keep right and descend to St Margaret's Bay where there are a pub, toilets and seats for eating your lunch.

Points of Interest Between Dover and Deal

Channel Swimmers Monument

Channel Swimmers Monument

The monument, on the waterfront, is an artwork entitled "On the Crest of a Wave" by Ray Smith. The blocks are made of Portland stone to represent the White Cliffs and the swimming figures, one leaving and one returning, are made of Kirkstone slate.

Dover is the most popular starting point for Channel swimmers. The first successful crossing was by Captain Matthew Webb in August 1875, taking 21 hours and 45 minutes. Jellyfish and currents had forced him to swim 39 miles, almost double the direct distance. The current record, set in 2012 by Australian Trent Grimsey, is 6 hours 55 minutes. Further east along the waterfront is a monument to Webb who died at the age of 35 attempting to swim across the Niagara Falls.

Dover Castle

One of England's finest, Dover castle dominates the town and is a significant landmark when approaching along the coast from either north or south. Within the castle site are an earlier church, possibly built by Canute, and a Roman lighthouse – one of two beacons that guided ships into the harbour, the foundations of the other surviving on the Western Heights.

While the Saxon plan of the Church of St Mary in Castro survives, the building itself has been much neglected over the centuries then unsympathetically restored in the 1860s and 1880s.

Both King Harold and William the Conqueror built earthwork fortifications here but the first stonework, including a curtain wall and the massive keep, was erected by Henry II between 1168 and 1186. Henry III added a further curtain wall but little else was done until around 1790 when much underground work was undertaken in anticipation of invasion by Napoleon.

During World War II the underground tunnelling was much extended. The 1940 evacuation of Dunkirk was planned and controlled from within the

over Castle

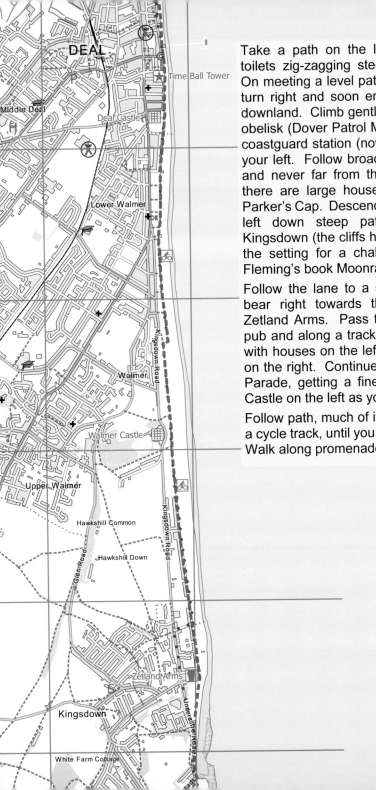

Take a path on the left just past the toilets zig-zagging steeply up the cliff. On meeting a level path at a T-junction, turn right and soon emerge onto open downland. Climb gently passing a large obelisk (Dover Patrol Memorial) and old coastguard station (now a tea room) on your left. Follow broad track parallel to and never far from the cliff edge until there are large houses on left at Old Parker's Cap. Descend past golf club on left down steep path to beach at Kingsdown (the cliffs here were used as the setting for a chalk cliff fall in Ian Fleming's book Moonraker).

Follow the lane to a small lay-by then bear right towards the shore at the Zetland Arms. Pass to the right of the pub and along a track becoming a path with houses on the left and sand dunes on the right. Continue along Wellington Parade, getting a fine view of Walmer Castle on the left as you pass.

Follow path, much of it side by side with a cycle track, until you pass Deal Castle. Walk along promenade to the pier.

tunnels ("Operation Dynamo") as was a decoy invasion to distract attention from the real D-Day landings. During the 1950s to 1970s the tunnels were equipped in readiness to become a local seat of government in the event of nuclear war.

Bleriot Memorial

In the shadow of the castle is a granite silhouette of the aeroplane in which Louis Bleriot was the first to fly across the Channel on 25 July 1909, marking the spot where he landed.

Bleriot Memorial

National Trust Visitor Centre

Reached after the stiff climb out of Dover, the visitor centre offers toilets, refreshments and views along with parking (at a charge to non-members) for those wishing to walk the cliffs without the climb.

The landscape around the centre is very much man-made. The car park above the centre was once the site of a prison. As you proceed north the broad, inclined track below coming up from the harbour once carried a railway. Much of the material for the construction of Dover harbour was excavated from the cliffs.

ormer Railway

Fan Bay Deep Shelter

The cliffs between Folkestone and Kingsdown were the front line for much of World War II. As well as the sound mirrors and gun emplacements there are many underground sites, largely buried. At Fan Bay the National Trust has removed a huge quantity of infill from one of these sites and opened it up to the public. The route passes the entrance but anyone wishing to visit should book in advance, either on-line or at the visitor centre (if tickets are still available for that

A Tour of the Fan Bay Deep Shelter

South Foreland Lighthouse

day). The excavation also uncovered two sound mirrors from World War I that had been buried for decades and can now be seen from the clifftop path looking back and down after passing the entrance.

South Foreland Lighthouse

This National Trust property is accessible on foot either from the visitor centre or from St Margaret's Bay. It is possible to access by road but for dropping off only as there is no visitor parking. The lighthouse once played a key role in warning ships away from the treacherous Goodwin Sands.

The Pines Gardens

As you enter St Margaret's Bay you pass this garden and eco-friendly wedding venue on your left and a cafe and World War II museum on your right. There is a 9 ft tall bronze statue of Winston Churchill made by Oscar Neman in 1972.

St Margaret's Bay

The white house ("White Cliffs") at the north end of the Bay was the seaside home of Noel Coward until 1952 and then of Ian Fleming and his wife Anna.

Dover Patrol Memorial

The obelisk is a prominent landmark as you approach St Margaret's Bay from either south or north. You pass it soon after reaching the clifftop having climbed steeply out of the village heading for Deal. It was completed in 1921 to commemorate the men of the Dover Patrol who died in the First World War. The main purpose of the patrol was to prevent German ships, including submarines, from using the English Channel and so force them to take a much longer route north of Scotland to reach the Atlantic. There are similar obelisks on the French coast and overlooking New York harbour.

The nearby coastguard lookout station has been turned into the Bluebirds Tea Rooms, no doubt influenced by the song made famous by Vera Lynn in 1942: "There'll be bluebirds over the white cliffs of Dover…". No one seems to know quite what the reference to bluebirds signifies, however. Opening times are restricted so don't rely on refreshment here without checking first.

Walmer Castle

One of three castles built by Henry VIII in 1538-40 when the Pope was encouraging Francis I of France to invade and restore the Pope's authority over the English church. Walmer Castle has long been the home of the Lords Warden of the Cinque Ports (see page 29). It is owned by English

Heritage and has an excellent tea room. Originally the sea came right up to the foot of the castle.

Walmer Castle

The intimate and informal feel to Walmer Castle, and especially the gardens, owes much to the efforts of Lady Hester Stanhope. Estranged from her eccentric father Lord Stanhope, known as "Citizen Stanhope" because of his sympathy for the French Revolution, she managed the household of her uncle William Pitt the Younger while, as Lord Warden of the Cinque Ports, he lived at Walmer between his periods of office as Prime Minister. When he returned to office in 1804 she assumed a similar role in Downing Street. After Pitt's death in 1806 she travelled to the Middle East, settling in the mountains of Lebanon. There she engaged in political intrigue and possibly espionage, particularly during the Napoleonic Wars that provoked so much fortification along the Kent coast, exerting considerable influence over local politics until her death in 1839.

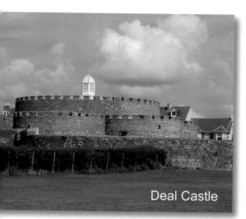
Deal Castle

Deal Castle

Another of Henry VIII's three castles, also owned by English Heritage and open to the public. Later alterations to accommodate the Captain of the Cinque Ports were destroyed by a German bomb in World War II and the castle has been restored to its original condition. Just south of the castle is the site where Julius Caesar is said to have landed in 55 BC but there is little evidence to substantiate such a precisely identified location.

Time Ball Tower

The tower has a sliding ball on its roof, installed in 1855 to signal the time to passing ships. It was connected electrically to the similar structure at the Royal Greenwich Observatory and would be raised each day just before 1 pm, being dropped exactly on the hour. The time ball mechanism has recently been restored to working order and can be visited in summer.

Time Ball Tower

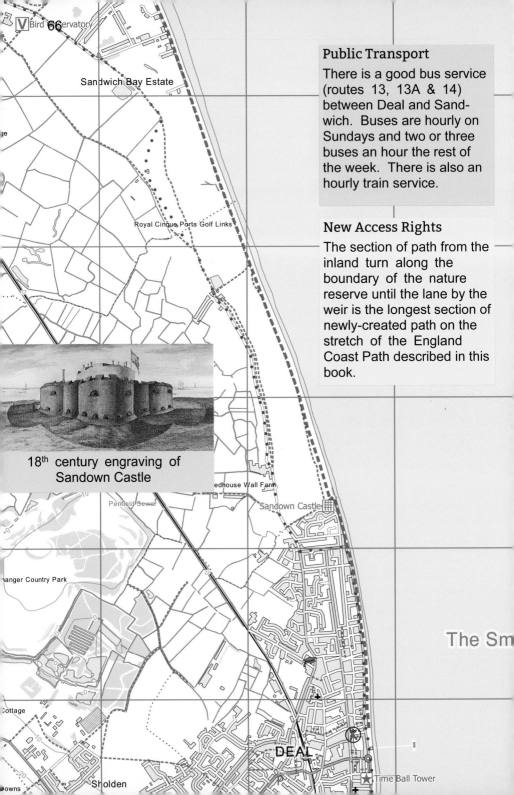

V Bird Observatory

Sandwich Bay Estate

Royal Cinque Ports Golf Links

18th century engraving of
Sandown Castle

edhouse Wall Farm

Penfield Sewer

Sandown Castle

anger Country Park

ottage

owns

Sholden

DEAL

The Sm

Time Ball Tower

Public Transport

There is a good bus service
(routes 13, 13A & 14)
between Deal and Sand-
wich. Buses are hourly on
Sundays and two or three
buses an hour the rest of
the week. There is also an
hourly train service.

New Access Rights

The section of path from the
inland turn along the
boundary of the nature
reserve until the lane by the
weir is the longest section of
newly-created path on the
stretch of the England
Coast Path described in this
book.

Section 7: Deal to Sandwich (10.2 miles)

Start at Deal pier and head north along the sea front. When the sea wall ends at a grassy triangle, note the rather fragmentary remains of Sandown castle. Continue north along a stony track adjacent to the shingle beach with the Royal Cinque Ports golf course on your left. Initially there is also a footpath on the left at the foot of the embankment which is softer under foot but lacks the sea view. A mile north of Sandown castle a path on the left offers the opportunity of a short inland detour to the Chequers Inn.

Continue along the beach-top path to the Sandwich Bay Estate where an asphalt track begins and you can marvel at the mock architecture copied from a range of periods. Follow the track, Princes Drive, northwards, now with the Royal St George's golf course on your left.

At a car park on the right there is a choice.

For a quick route to Sandwich (reducing the distance by about 4 miles) continue along Princes Drive for a short distance then bear left at the entrance to the The Lodge (formerly the Prince's Golf Course Clubhouse and now an accommodation block and restaurant for the Club) and left again along a well-defined track. When this track starts to curve right, go straight ahead along good path passing the left hand end of a hedge. Continue in the same direction passing the left hand corner of the hedged boundary of a garden to meet a lane at a corner where you rejoin the official route of the coast path.

Cross the lane to a path just left of the corner leading across a weir then continue as in the last two sentences below.

To follow the full route of the coast path, go through the car park and take a sandy track heading north past an information board between The Lodge on the left and dunes and the sea on the right. Pass the new Prince's Golf Course Clubhouse 250 metres to your left.

On reaching an information board and a kissing gate ahead into the Nature Reserve, turn left inland with the reserve fence on your right. Follow path as it twists and turns around edge of golf course and over a couple of bridges then along edge of woodland. Over third bridge turn right along bottom of embankment, again following twists and turns until path crosses stony track and turns right along top of embankment. At end turn left then right along stony track: watch for right turn up to river embankment with view of Discovery Park on far side. Turn left and follow track along top of embankment to lane. Turn right across a weir then along the bank of the river Stour. Follow the path, keeping right at all junctions, into Sandwich.

68

Stippled area is the Sandwich and Pegwell Bay National Nature Reserve

Sandwich Flats

Black Sand Point

Flagstaff Road

Prince's Clubhouse

Prince's Golf Links

Great Stonar

Bloody Point

Discovery Park

Ramsgate Road

A256 Ramsgate Road

Sandwic

Sandwich

Prince's Golf Links

The Lodge

Stonar Lake

New Downs Farm Cottage

The New Cut

Royal St George's Golf Links

Royal St George's Clubhouse

Princes Drive

WICH

Sandwich

Vigo Spring

Toll

Bird Observatory

The Delf

Poll Bay Dike

Poll Bay Dike

Sandwich Bay Estate

Points of Interest Between Deal and Sandwich

Deal

Deal

Although the reputed landing place of Julius Caesar in both 55 BC and 54 BC, Deal was no more than a small fishing village by the time of the Domesday book. As the Stour at Sandwich silted up, Deal assumed greater importance as a port and became a Cinque Port as a limb of Sandwich. Thomas Becket landed here in 1170 on return from exile as did Perkin Warbeck when attempting an invasion in 1495. William Penn sailed from Deal for America in 1682. After the closure of the dockyard in 1863 the town became mainly a seaside resort. The buildings facing the sea front north of the pier give a very fine impression although opinions vary as to their age some suggesting 17th and 18th century origin and others that most buildings are 19th century or later.

Deal Pier

The current pier was opened in 1957 and has been designed very much with the sea angler in mind. There are opportunities for angling along the main stem of the pier and a lower section at the end for casting out into deeper water. An original iron pier was opened in 1864 but damaged so badly in World War II that it had to be replaced.

Deal Pier

Sandown Castle

The third of Henry VIII's castles, its original plan almost identical to Walmer's, Sandown Castle is now marked by little more than a rockery. It was undermined by the sea and largely demolished for safety reasons in 1859.

Royal Cinque Ports Golf Club

Twice a host to the British Open, this course was laid out in 1892. It is not now used for the Open because of its susceptibility to flooding at exceptionally high tides.

Sandwich Bay Estate

A private estate for the wealthy, begun in 1912 by the Earl of Guilford and including houses by celebrated architects such as Sir Edwin Lutyens. The White House was once the constituency home of Jonathan Aitken, then MP for South Thanet and Chief Secretary to the Treasury. He famously fell from grace after being convicted for perjury and imprisoned over the matter of who paid a hotel bill and had to sell the house to help pay his legal expenses.

Sandwich Bay Esta

Another house on the estate, Rest Harrow, was built in 1910 for Lord Astor and his wife Nancy, the first woman to take a seat in the House of Commons.

Bird Observatory

The Sandwich Bay Bird Observatory is half a mile inland along the first path on the left after you leave the Sandwich Bay Estate heading north. If visiting by road you will have to use the toll road into the Sandwich Bay Estate but if visiting only the Observatory you should be charged a reduced toll (at the time of writing just £1 compared with a full charge of £7). As well as much information about birds you can get refreshment and very reasonably priced accommodation.

Royal St George's Golf Club

Ian Fleming was a member and used the course as the setting for an encounter between James Bond and Auric Goldfinger, although he changed the name slightly to Royal St Marks.

Prince's Golf Club

The course was originally completed in 1906 on land donated by the Earl of Guilford. Host to the British Open in 1932 it was almost obliterated during World War II and has been substantially redesigned.

Sandwich and Pegwell Bay National Nature Reserve

The Salutation

The entrance is on your left as you enter Sandwich. The house, now a hotel, was designed by Edwin Lutyens and built in 1911 for Henry Farrar whose family owned the Westminster Bank. The gardens, open to the public, were laid out by Gertrude Jekyll.

The Goodwin Sands

Lying four miles offshore from Deal, the Goodwin Sands have been a hazard to shipping for many centuries. They are said to be named after the Saxon Earl Godwin, father of King Harold.

In November 1703 a storm drove four English warships onto the sandbar with the loss of 1500 sailors. It was claimed that many of the citizens of Deal were too busy looting the wrecked ships to support an attempt to rescue the sailors stranded on the Sands, so that only 200 were saved. Despite the North and South Foreland lighthouses and up to four lightships, ships continued to founder on the sand bar for much of the twentieth century. In 1954 one of the lightships was driven from its moorings with the loss of the crew of seven.

In 1854 a cricket match was played on the sands at low tide and the event has been repeated from time to time.

In 2012 proposals were published to build an international hub airport on the sands to avoid the need for expansion of Heathrow or Gatwick but so far the idea has not been taken forward.

The sands are constantly shifting so that some of the many wrecks, including a German U-boat from World War II and two American ships lost in 1946, disappear and reappear at irregular intervals.

Engraving of the Goodwin Sands during the 1703 storm

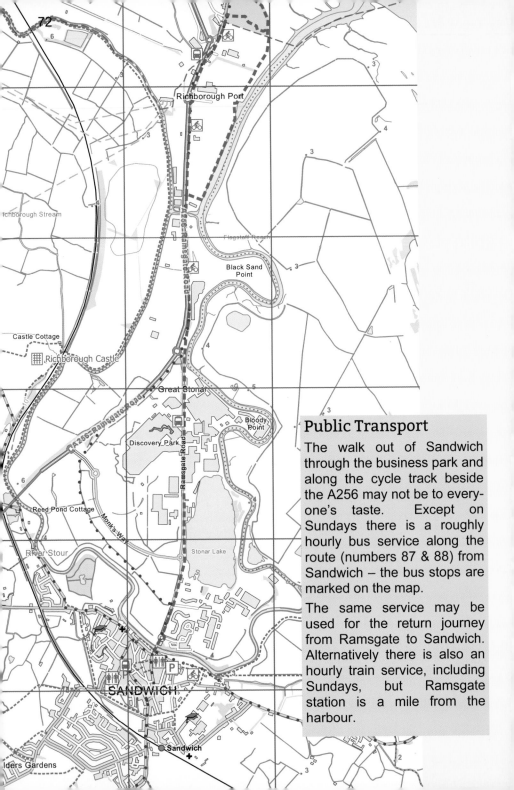

Richborough Port

Ichborough Stream

Flagstaff Reach

Black Sand
Point

Castle Cottage

Richborough Castle

Great Stonar

A256 Ramsgate Road

A256 Ramsgate Road

Ramsgate Road

Discovery Park

Bloody
Point

Reed Pond Cottage

Monk's Way

River Stour

Stonar Lake

SANDWICH

Sandwich

Iders Gardens

Public Transport

The walk out of Sandwich through the business park and along the cycle track beside the A256 may not be to everyone's taste. Except on Sundays there is a roughly hourly bus service along the route (numbers 87 & 88) from Sandwich – the bus stops are marked on the map.

The same service may be used for the return journey from Ramsgate to Sandwich. Alternatively there is also an hourly train service, including Sundays, but Ramsgate station is a mile from the harbour.

Section 8: Sandwich to Ramsgate (6.9 miles)

Start at the quayside in Sandwich and cross the swing bridge heading north past mini-roundabout. Pass the Sandwich Industrial Estate on the right. At roundabout go straight ahead with Stonar Lake on other side of fence on the right. Carry on through the Discovery Park to junction with the A256 at roundabout and bear right along cycle track.

The official route as approved by the Secretary of State leaves the road soon after the Stonar Cut, indicated by sluice on right, and follows the quayside at Richborough Port. However, this section of path had to be created for the purposes of the coast path and the landowner objected. The dispute was taken to a public hearing at which the Inspector supported the proposed route but advised that it should be closed when the quayside is needed for the landowner's business of vehicle storage. As the landowner's need has become virtually continuous, you will probably be unable to use the quayside and will have to continue along the cycle track to the petrol station and sandwich shop.

Keep right at roundabout along Sandwich Road. Opposite entrance to golf range go through gate on right. Do not turn left along the cycle track but go straight ahead, keeping right at all junctions, to the edge of the estuary. Here you join the new but probably unavailable path along the Port

emerging on the right. Turn left along the edge of Stonelees Reserve and at a kissing gate enter Pegwell Bay Country Park. Turn right and follow seaward boundary of Country Park and Nature Reserve past car park to Sandwich Road.

Turn right along the cycle track, skirting round the back of a petrol station, and passing the Viking ship. At entrance to picnic area bear right to path at far corner and follow across asphalt track – the site of the old Hoverport is visible – and along the water's edge to Pegwell. Turn right to corner by seafront then bear left past some public houses then left again uphill until red brick wall on the right comes to an end. Turn sharp right downhill to seafront. Turn left along path through park to meet road. Continue along road above marina. At the end of the marina look for the large obelisk where the walk finishes.

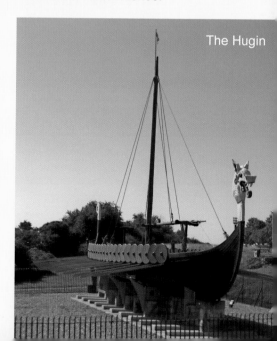

The Hugin

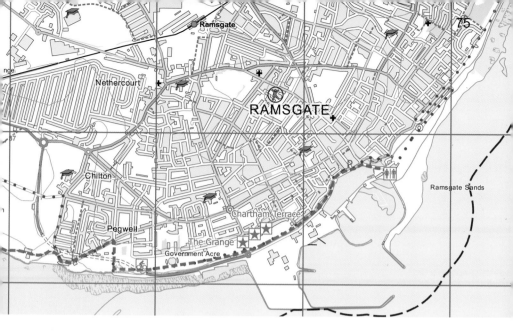

Points of Interest between Sandwich and Ramsgate

Sandwich

The port was originally established to control shipping through the Wantsum Channel which carried most continental traffic bound for London. By the end of the Hundred Years War in 1453 it was the most important naval base in the country and a "head" Cinque Port but thereafter the gradual silting up of harbour and surrounding area led to a steady decline. The town's fortunes were revived by the arrival of Huguenot refugees who set up cloth-making businesses – the refugees started arriving in 1561 and by 1574 there were 2400 of them making up half the town's population.

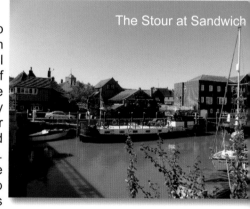

The Stour at Sandwich

Barbican Gate

Built in 1539 this twin turreted gate looks across the swing bridge by which you leave the town at the start of your journey to Ramsgate. The swing bridge is still in use and will be opened free of charge for any vessel too tall to go under it provided that an hour's notice is given.

Discovery Park

Discovery Park

This business park used to be Pfizer's research, development and manufacturing centre where many drugs were discovered including Viagra. Since Pfizer's departure the new owners have sought to create a centre for high tech businesses and research and development companies.

Stonar

The name comes from a long-gone mediaeval port. A strip of land barely 200 metres wide separates two sections of the Stour that are over 6 miles apart by boat. There is now a cutting that, when the sluice gates are open, allows water to bypass those 6 miles and hence also Sandwich if the flow is great enough to risk flooding the town.

Richborough Port

In 1916 a huge military depot was built here for transporting men and equipment to the Continent. During the Second World Way it was again

Pegwell Bay

used as a base for transporting goods and in particular was where parts of the Mulberry harbours (see page 35) were constructed.

Pegwell Bay

The bay and the Stour estuary are popular with a wide variety of waterfowl, especially oystercatchers. There are nature reserves both north and south of the river mouth. The bay was a popular landing site for those invading Britain until William the Conqueror broke the pattern by landing in Sussex.

Richborough Castle

Not really a castle but a Roman fort. When the Roman commander Aulus Plautius landed in 43 AD he established a supply base here fortified with earthworks. At this time the site was separated from the island of Thanet by the Wantsum Channel and indeed may have been itself a small island. As the invasion of Britain proceeded tens, perhaps hundreds, of thousands of troops from the continent disembarked here then marched westward along Watling Street to London and beyond. Soon the military earthworks were flattened and the large settlement of Rutupiae built – the town was much larger than site enclosed by the current wall. There was an amphitheatre across the road to the south but this has not been excavated and cannot be visited.

As the Roman Empire declined and Britain came under attack from Saxon raiders there was a significant retrenchment. It was then, around 285 AD, that the currently visible walls were built and Rutupiae became one of a series of Saxon Shore forts built to defend Britain against the raiders (hence the Saxon Shore Way that follows the line of forts).

There was another fort at Reculver, at the other end of the Wantsum Channel, that lies on a future section of the Kent Coast Path.

Richborough Fort

Richborough was said to be famous throughout the Roman Empire for the quality of the local oysters.

St Augustine's Cross

The Saxon-style cross, erected in 1884, marks the traditional landing place of St Augustine in 597 when the location was still on the coast - it is now half a mile inland. He was greeted by King Ethelbert who insisted on meeting in the open air as he feared Augustine's magic which he believed was effective only within buildings. Despite his suspicions, Etherlbert converted to Christianity along with thousands of his subjects.

Viking Ship

The "Hugin" is a replica of a traditional Viking ship and was sailed by 53 Danes from Denmark to Thanet in 1949 to mark the 1500th anniversary of the Viking invasion of Britain. The invaders, led by supposed brothers Hengist and Horsa, came ashore in 449 at the same spot that St Augustine subsequently landed.

Hands and Molecule

This sculpture by David Barnes was unveiled to mark the opening of the Thanet cycle route in 2000. It was funded by Pfizer, then still operating in Sandwich, to celebrate the many innovative products developed in East Kent.

The Grange and St Augustine's Church

The Grange was designed and built by Augustus Pugin as his family home.

Hands and Molecule

Pugin was responsible for designing much of the interior of the Palace of Westminster and for creating the Victorian Gothic style in architecture. Next to The Grange stands St Augustine's church, also designed and built by Pugin.

Restored by the Landmark Trust to its appearance in the 1840s, The Grange is not open to the public but is available for holiday letting through the Trust and for guided tours of certain rooms by appointment, at the time of writing on Wednesday afternoons.

Chartham Terrace

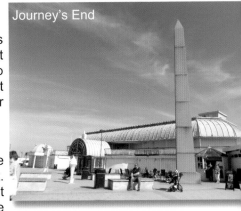
Journey's End

Immediately east of St Augustine's church stands Chartham Terrace, built by architect Matthew Habersham to rival Pugin's creations. Some say it was built so close to the church in order to annoy Pugin.

Ramsgate

Starting as a fishing village, Ramsgate found success as a Regency resort. Most guidebooks have little, or at least little that is kind, to say about Ramsgate yet it has a fine harbour and plenty of Georgian architecture. Many notable people have holidayed here, including Karl Marx, Charles Darwin and Princess Victoria. Van Gogh lived here when working as a language master before taking up painting as a career. The large obelisk that marks the end of our route was erected in 1822 to commemorate George IV's trip to Hanover via the town.

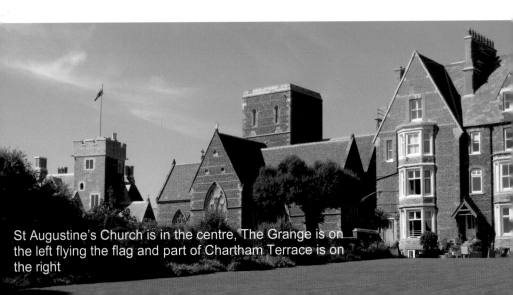
St Augustine's Church is in the centre, The Grange is on the left flying the flag and part of Chartham Terrace is on the right

About the Ramblers

The Ramblers has been championing the interests of walkers, encouraging more people to go walking and protecting the places we walk since 1935.

We promote walking as both a pleasurable activity and as something that brings huge physical and mental health benefits to those who participate.

Our members enjoy a range of benefits, including 48,000 led walks organised by almost 500 local groups across Great Britain, access to 2,500 downloadable Ramblers Routes and our quarterly magazine, *Walk*. All walkers, from those who tackle challenging long distance trails to dog walkers exploring their local neighbourhood, benefit from the work we do.

The England Coast Path, of which the route described in this book is a part, was possible because of the vision, campaigning skills and hard work of Ramblers' staff and volunteers.

The right to roam across open mountain, moorland and similar terrain also came about because of persistent campaigning by the Ramblers.

Every day our volunteers scrutinise proposals from landowners and others to close or alter public rights of way to ensure that any changes do not disadvantage walkers.

And our local path maintenance teams clear overgrown paths and install stiles, gates and steps to help keep paths accessible and enable people to go walking in the places that they love.

Even this book represents hundreds of hours of work by Ramblers' volunteers.

There are so many reasons to join the Ramblers and help us to continue to create a Britain where everyone has the freedom to enjoy the outdoors on foot and benefit from the experience. Find out more about what you can do to support the Ramblers today at www.ramblers.org.uk.

Acknowledgements

Photographs

All photographs not listed below were taken by Robert Peel.

Pages 6 & 7: All images supplied by Ramblers' Central Office

Page 23: Marsh Frog: Marie-Lan Nguyen, Wikimedia Commons

Page 56: 1915 derailment: source unknown

Mapping

Contains OS data © Crown copyright and database rights (2015)

The base mapping is derived from Ordnance Survey data released into the public domain under the Open Government Licence.

The rights of way in East Sussex are derived from data released into the public domain by East Sussex County Council.

The rights of way in Kent are reproduced by kind permission of Kent County Council under OS licence number 26022016.

The national and regional cycle networks are reproduced by kind permission of Sustrans.

Some maps contain National Nature Reserve data © Natural England copyright 2014.

The route of the coast path is based on GPS tracks and the personal observations of the authors.

All other information on the maps has been created by the authors.

Other

The authors are grateful for the assistance and cooperation of Natural England and Kent County Council in producing this guide. Any errors, however, are those of the authors.

Ramsgate Harbour